Keys to the Truculent Me

And Other Things That Drive Me Crazy

John Branning

Keys to the Truculent Me

Copyright © 2017 by John Branning

All rights reserved.

John Branning

Winthrop ME 04364

"Sinking Relation-ship" originally appeared in the July 13, 2016 online edition of Defenestration Magazine.

First Printing: September 2017
Pusillanimous Books

www.JohnBranning.com

ISBN: 978-0-9970773-1-5

Nothing can confound a wise man more than laughter from a dunce.

-- *Lord Byron*

Or, perhaps, this book. But you paid for it, so who's laughing now?

Contents

Intro

I published my first anthology of humor columns as an ebook in 2015. SHAMELESS SELF-PROMOTION: **Selfie-Facing** -- *Analog Musings in a Digital World* is available for a modest sum from the usual online sources – or, if you prefer, I'll leave you a series of voicemails, reading one entry at a time, for free. I was not sufficiently scarred by the process of assembling Book Number One to dissuade me from now delivering Book Number Two. How's this for an opening sentence?:

- "Thank you for your interest in my second book."

Very Hemingway-esque, *n'est ce-pas*? Simple, direct, unadorned, sleep-inducing.

The book part is easy -- the only place where I'm stuck is the title. I'm considering the following and would love to get your opinion:

- **Premature Articulation** -- *Speaking Before Thinking: The Donald J. Trump Story*
- **A Love for the Ages** -- *Taylor Swift and Her Beaus*
- **Rumpus Room** -- *The Kardashian Saga*
- **If The Facts Don't Fit The Theory, Change The Facts** -- *Einstein's Prescient Insights into Kellyanne Conway's Thought Process*
- **Opie-oid Addiction** -- *What I Learned From Binge-Watching 'The Andy Griffith Show'*
- **Kraut Control** -- *Leadership Lessons from Angela Merkel*
- **Maple Stirrup** --*The Life of a Canadian Cowboy*
- **Iceberg Lettuce Alone** -- *Climate Change Deniers Find Themselves Adrift*
- **I'll Have a Dark & Stormy** -- *Edward Bulwer-Lytton Bellies Up to the Bar*

Actually, now that I reflect on the above I guess this second attempt may present more challenges than first anticipated. If you've read **Selfie-Facing** (see SHAMELESS SELF-PROMOTION above), you may have at least noticed, if not been offended by, the casual and frequent use of profanity in it. However, in my attempts to reach a wider audience (i.e., in the double-digits) with this next screed, I've attempted to dial it back to a PG-13 from the first book's hard R. In order to make that clear to the masses, let's instead consider one of the following titles:

- **F-Balm**
- **Swear Are You?**
- **Live and Let Expletive**
- **Curses! Roiled Again**
- **Just Between Cuss**
- **I Had A Blasphemy Last Night**
- **How I Spent My Summer Imprecation**
- **Now I've Obscene Everything**

Hmm... on third thought (and quickly approaching my limit), I think I'll stick with the title that appears on the cover of what you're reading right now (which, I hope, is not "REMAINDERED"). As my inspiration Hemingway once said, "You shouldn't write if you can't write." I'm trying to make sense of that, but I swear this is one instance where Ernest may be full of shiitake.

Anyway -- this copy of [INSERT FINAL TITLE HERE] you're holding in your hands / reading on your tablet / squinting at on your phone collects a sample of my posts from November 2015 until about ten minutes before this all went to the printer's. You can read everything I wrote before, during and after that time frame (but for God's sake, why would you want to? Even my wife and son can't be bothered) on my blog, <u>Facts Optional</u>, which can be found at www.JohnBranning.com.

If you're a fan of puns, non-sequiturs, and self-deprecating humor -- you may find this book amusing. If you're not, then every day must be a real drag for you.

Section 1: Transmission Trouble

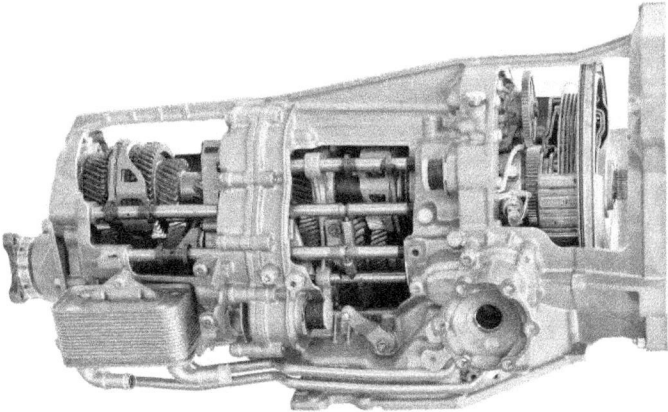

Rude Awakening

This morning my sleep was ended not by the ringing of the alarm clock but by my wife Carol punching me in the nose.

As I cried out in pain, she offered this: "Oh, I'm so sorry -- I didn't think you were still in bed."

"So -- you just struck out blindly, not checking to see if there was still a head nestled atop the other pillow? Because I can assure you there was, and now there is a throbbing and perhaps damaged nose affixed to that head."

"I *said* I was sorry," she replied in what I considered to be a tone devoid of contrition. At this point, I got up and went downstairs into the bathroom to see if my nose was broken or bleeding. It wasn't, but from the force of the wayward blow Carol delivered it very well might have been.

The perpetrator then came downstairs and asked if I'd made coffee yet. I stood speechless for a few moments, incredulous that while I was still recovering from my injury, at her hand, her thoughts were only of breakfast. Then I placed a filter in the basket and started the coffee.

Carol emerged from the shower twenty minutes later, opening the bathroom door to let the steam escape. I said I needed to come in and use the toilet; she responded by asking if I could wait a minute or two. Well, perhaps a few years ago I could have, but these days I find it prudent to address the urge as quickly as possible. I informed her as such; she shot a quick but obviously annoyed glance my way and after a beat moved aside so I could get past. People offer many indications of how well matched they are as a couple -- shared interest in gardening, mutual love of travel, engaging in spirited political debate, sexual compatibility -- but I think the ultimate barometer of spousal longevity is willingness, however grudging, to share the bathroom when one of you requires time on the can.

After Carol left for work I still felt drained from the morning's events and decided to slip back under the covers to make up for the sleep I'd been robbed of due to the assault at dawn. As I settled into a comfortable position our cat Nate jumped up on the bed and demanded attention. I tried to shoo him away and he responded by poking me in the nose with a needle-sharp claw. I leapt out of bed and ran downstairs to, for the second time that morning, check for damage to my nose. While the puncture was small, it bled for some time and when it finally stopped it looked as though I'd just had my right nostril pierced.

Since the bedroom was no longer a safe haven, I poured myself the last of the coffee and went into the living room to watch the noontime news. No sooner had I settled into the couch than another of our cats, Miles, jumped into my lap and began to head-butt me. I tried to shoo him away and he responded by poking me in the scrotum with a needle-sharp claw. I leapt off the couch and ran into the bathroom to, for the third time that day, check for damage to my person; I feared he may have vasectomized me. Such a procedure may, at this stage of my life, be superfluous but you know what some people say: they feel safer sleeping with a loaded gun, even if they never intend to use it.

By now I'd given up on the idea of getting any further rest and decided to make a fresh start to the day with a shower. After stepping out of the tub I was greeted by the last of our cats, Sophie, who has a foot fetish and loves to rub her face all over my bare feet when they are freshly scrubbed. I tried to shoo her away and she responded by clinging to my ankle with all of her needle-sharp claws. Since I was already in the bathroom there really wasn't any place for me to escape to, so I stood there screeching until Sophie decided to let go and saunter back to her kibble. She'd left a series of red, raw scratches circling my lower leg, creating a dotted line that will be a helpful guide for the orthopedist when my foot eventually requires amputation once the infection sets in.

By the time I'd dried off, treated this most recent wound, gotten dressed and waited for the pain to subside, the day was more or less shot. I made myself a vodka tonic and tried, unsuccessfully, to work up any enthusiasm to prepare the evening meal. Thankfully, frozen pizza was invented for just this reason. Carol returned from work and walked through the door just as the oven timer rang. I reached in to remove the pizza and accidentally brushed the back of my hand against the upper rack, causing an immediate and painful singe.

"What's that smell?" Carol asked. "Did you burn the pizza?" I stood speechless for a few moments, incredulous that as I recovered from yet another injury her thoughts were only of dinner. Then I pulled the pizza from the oven and served her a slice.

After eating I pled exhaustion and announced I was going to bed. I stood, able to rise only to a crouch, with breath whistling through the extra hole in the side of my nose and, favoring my good leg, hobbled upstairs. Carol came in later, cradling me in her arms while whispering how sorry she was for my ailments and offering hope I'd feel better. I nodded my head and offered a slight grunt of acknowledgment.

Carol ended this very trying day for me on such a sweet note that, before drifting off to sleep, I nearly felt remorse for stuffing catnip in her pillow and resetting her alarm clock two hours early. Fortunately, it's her turn to make the coffee tomorrow morning.

To Speech His Own

Welcome to Part XXIV of my series, "Learn How To Better Espresso Yourself Through Proper Word Choosing." In today's lessen, we will review the Parts of Speech and how to combine those parts into a hole.

There are somewhere between six and a gazillion parts of speech, depending on how you categorize them. For this lesion, we'll go with what I have listed below. If you have any modifications or additions to this list you'd like to suggest, please email me at stuffitinasock@whocares.net.

The Parts of Speech are:

Nouns

A noun is defined as being a *person, place* or *thing*. Examples of each:

- Person: the *President-elect*, a *xenophobe*; the *milkman* (since both *milk* and *man* are nouns, "milkman" is referred to as a "renoun," mostly because of the rumors he fathered several children in the neighborhood).
- Place: My father often said he would like to put me in my *place*. I'd respond with "Where -- a *volcano?* The *supermarket? Moosewood Lake?*" He'd reply, "How about the *hospital?*"
- Thing: This one is easy since there are many *things* -- this *thing* over here; that *thing* we were just talking about; "That *Thing* You Do;" let me *thing* about it for a while.

A *proper name* is a noun -- "Hey, *Jim!*" An *improper name* is also a noun -- "Hey, Jim! You *shithead!*"

In later lessons, we'll get into further depth about sub-categorization of nouns -- abstract, collective, and wait until we talk about the Seven Mutant Plurals! (I believe at least five of them were featured in the last *X-Men* movie.)

Pronouns

A pronoun replaces a noun. To illustrate:

- "In high school, my girlfriend Gail informed me she'd be going to the senior prom with *Jim Delaney* instead of me."

Replacing a noun, especially one who showered his girlfriend with flowers and unrelenting affection, and particularly with a shithead like Jim Delaney, can be devastating.

Verbs

Verbs describe an *action* or *state.* This can be a little confusing since you might think *Maine* and *New Hampshire* are places and therefore nouns, but apparently they are actually verbs. What can I say? Grammar is a rough business. I don't make the rules; I just follow them.

When we talk about verbs we also must talk about *tense.* This is understandable because the election results have left many of us feeling that way.

As a side note, one of my favorite vocal groups back in the day was Peaches and Verb. They sang "Shake Your Groove Thing" -- in that song title, *Shake* is a verb and *Your* is a possessive pronoun, but what is *Groove? Groove* is like "the boogie" -- you'll know it when you feel it.

Modifiers

There are two basic kinds of modifiers, *adverbs* and *adjectives:*

- *Adverbs* modify verbs. If we were to insert an adverb into the sentence, "See Jack run," in order to modify the verb *run,* we might say, "See Jack run. *No running inside the house, Jack!*" In that way, we would modify Jack's action.
- *Adjectives* modify nouns or pronouns. As an example: "Upon hearing he was planning to take my girlfriend to the prom, I *beat the shit* out of the pronoun *Jim Delaney.*" I

certainly modified his face, but Gail still wouldn't go to the prom with me.

Preposition

Prepositions are very common words, such as *in, at, on, by, before* and *multitudinous*. Let's use one in a sentence: "I've got a *preposition* for you, Delaney -- leave Gail alone or I'm going to modify your face."

Conjunction

I had *conjunction* once and was out of work for three days. Symptoms include red, itchy eyes and a very unappealing discharge.

Interjection

An interjection is what I was hoping would happen after attending the senior prom with my girlfriend Gail. As you may have inferred, that plan did not come to fruition.
--

In our next lesson, we'll explore how to choose between *that* versus *which, who* versus *whom, love* versus *infatuation*, and how to put up with relative pronouns during the holiday season.

Like many of you, I am often drained after getting home at the end of a busy day, exhausted from fulfilling my role as the least-productive member of my team at work, and find myself facing the challenge of preparing a nutritious and appealing dinner for the family. Selecting a recipe, scouring the refrigerator and cupboards for all the ingredients, sharpening the knives, peeling the potatoes, butchering the hog... sometimes everyone else has headed off to bed before I am ready to serve the evening meal at 10:45 P.M. Then the next challenge is waking everyone up and dragging them back to the table to eat.

There are numerous videos online purporting to show easy-peasy recipes, with the illusion heightened by time-lapse photography. "Here are red and green bell peppers / (chop-chop-chop) / And now they're seeded and diced into identical bite-sized sections." "Pop open a can of prepared bread dough / (smoosh-smoosh-smoosh) / Ta-da! Beef Wellington!" If you slow any of these videos down to real-time, you'll find they take 20 times more effort than the hyper-speed version you were just suckered by.

Even the cooking shows on TV are misleading. They are all hosted by professional chefs, using top-notch tools, boundless resources, and possessing a certain *savoir-faire* in the kitchen. What about those of us who are working with dull knives, a gouged cutting board, and the only spices found on the lazy susan are a three-year-old shaker of oregano and a half-bottle of Gravy Master passed down from your grandmother? What tips are there for the home cook who is only *faire-enough*?

I, and I alone, can help you separate the white from the yolk. Let me disabuse you of some common fallacies around simplifying dinner time:

"Many hands make light work." This proverb may be true, but it applies to the kitchen only when you are demolishing it as part of a home renovation project. If you try to get your family -- especially any children age 12 or younger -- involved with meal preparation, it will take you three times as long to complete and a sticky mess will be spread out to the virtual horizon. Your kitchen is too small for an army of amateur sous-chefs to be milling about. The key to success here is to usher everyone out of your way by sitting them down to watch reruns of *2 Broke Girls* with a package of rice cakes and bowls of raw pinto beans as snacks to tide them over until suppertime. After an hour or so spent sampling these unpalatable choices (both food and program), they'll be thankful for nearly anything you serve for dinner, including sautéed liver and even Brussels sprouts.

Make use of your crock pot. Again, a common misconception; there is nothing task- or time-saving about using a crock pot. Everyone thinks you can just dump a can of cream of mushroom soup on top of a whole chicken, splash it with some of the Zinfandel left over from the cheap bottle your cousin brought to guzzle from last Easter, set the timer, and come home to an incredible *coq au vin*. Nothing could be further from the truth; you'll return to find stringy chicken drowning in a pool of murky slime, and now you have to order a pizza. The only useful thing to do with that appliance is donate it to your local Goodwill -- you can take a tax write-off while clearing up valuable counter space. You think I'm kidding? Head over to Goodwill and see how many like-new crock pots they have on display.

Go vegetarian or (even worse) vegan. "Gee," you think to yourself one day, "if I had to shop only for vegetables, it would save me time in the store, and all I'd have to do is sauté a pan of hacked-up zucchini for dinner every night. What could be better?" Practically anything, that's what. If you've ever read a vegetarian or vegan cookbook, then you know that every other recipe calls for something called "tempeh." Tempeh is a fermented soy product offering protein and false promise. If you can even find it at your local supermarket, it's often more expensive per pound than beef, chicken or fish -- but, in fairness, it goes much farther. Often as far as the garbage can.

A strictly vegan diet is even more ridiculous; now your pantry will be filled with ingredients like chickpea flour, coconut oil, flax seeds, agave nectar, quinoa (pronounced, "ugh"), edamame and cashew milk. Want to know something tasty you can make from these ingredients? NOTHING. THERE IS NOTHING REMOTELY TASTY TO BE

MADE FROM THESE INGREDIENTS. Your hunger will have to be satiated by the sense of smug satisfaction you derive from conferring the rights of personhood on chickens, cows, and bees.

So what to do? Don't ask me; I'm weary from another trying day of failure at work. If one more person asks me, "What's for dinner?" I'm going to lose my tempeh.

Standing on the Alleged

I've just learned that Kim Kardashian, who largely removed herself from the public eye for a few months after allegedly being robbed in Paris, has returned to social media by posting two Instagram videos where she is allegedly shaking her "booty."

CORRECTION: Kim Kardashian has posted two Instagram videos where she is shaking her alleged "booty."

LET'S TRY ONCE MORE: Kim Kardashian has posted two Instagram videos where a "booty," allegedly hers, is being shaken.

NOPE, THAT WASN'T RIGHT EITHER: There does not appear to be any ancillary contribution to the shaking of said "booty." The shaking seems to be completely within the control of the person pictured in the videos, who may be Kim Kardashian or, it is alleged, perhaps one of her sisters, and whose "booty" is the body part in motion.

GETTING CLOSER: The Instagram videos that are alleged to show Kim Kardashian shaking her "booty" may mark her return to social media. In response to critics who claim this is a salacious re-emergence, the Kardashian camp responded that the videos were done in a tasteful manner since the "booty-shaking" appears in slow-motion, making it artistic and not at all lascivious.

HEY, NOW: I have just stumbled across a new word -- "concupiscent." That would have been a good one to use in the previous paragraph.

TO CONTINUE: There was also another picture posted on Instagram that included breasts resting upon a second "booty." As I write this, ownership of these body parts has not been firmly established, but because of the degree of concupiscence on display it is alleged all the parts are associated with at least two Kardashian family members. However, none of the parts are alleged to belong to either Kris or Caitlyn Jenner.

IN SUMMARY: Kim Kardashian, who is alleged to be a "famous celebrity," but is definitely someone for whom I have no use, continues to generate what I used to refer to as "fake news." Now, "fake news" is described as fiction posted online which is alleged to have influenced the outcome of the recent election and, as a result, the foundation of our democratic process has allegedly been undermined by the efforts of so-called state-sponsored "bad actors."

Speaking of "bad actors" -- that pretty much describes the Kardashians, doesn't it?

Speaking of "fiction posted online" -- that pretty much describes the T&A in those social media posts, doesn't it?

I am now nearly out of patience, allegations and quotation marks. Back to the (alleged) "real" news.

Bad Sports

"Average players want to be left alone. Good players want to be coached. Great players want to be told the truth." -- Doc Rivers

- **The truth is -- you suck.**

"It's not whether you get knocked down; it's whether you get up." -- Vince Lombardi

- **And also whether you file a complaint with OSHA.**

"A good hockey player plays where the puck is. A great hockey player plays where the puck is going to be." -- Wayne Gretzky

- **Where the puck were you yesterday?**

"If you have everything under control, you're not moving fast enough." -- Mario Andretti

- **This explains our CEO's chaotic leadership style.**

"Age is no barrier. It's a limitation you put on your mind." -- Jackie Joyner-Kersee

- **Then why do job applications want to know what year I graduated from college?**

"It isn't the mountains ahead to climb that wear you out; it's the pebble in your shoe." -- Muhammad Ali

- **Nevertheless, our dress code still prohibits flip-flops.**

"You can't put a limit on anything. The more you dream, the farther you get." -- Michael Phelps

- **But fall asleep just once during a presentation to upper management and next thing you know you're out on your keister.**

"Persistence can change failure into extraordinary achievement." -- Matt Biondi

- **It can also lead to a sexual harassment claim.**

"It's not the will to win that matters—everyone has that. It's the will to prepare to win that matters." -- Paul "Bear" Bryant

- **It also matters that you prepare your will before you permanently "leave the field".**

"What to do with a mistake: recognize it, admit it, learn from it, forget it." -- Dean Smith

- **Of course, I'm referring to my own mistakes here – one more screw up from <u>you</u> and you're out on your keister.**

"I've learned that something constructive comes from every defeat." -- Tom Landry

- **A pity our shareholders don't feel the same way.**

"Make sure your worst enemy doesn't live between your own two ears." -- Laird Hamilton

- **Perhaps you should try using Head & Shoulders.**

"It ain't over till it's over." – Yogi Berra

- **Oh, it's over – you can pick up your packet from HR on the way out.**

Catamaran Away

We're finally getting some warm weather again, so when I got home from work the other day I wanted to open things up to let the refreshing lake breeze pass through the house to cool things down. The storm door at one entrance has a nifty slide-down panel that reveals a half-screen, and then I opened the French door on the deck side of the house where a sliding screen is in place to keep the bugs out and the cats in. With that task accomplished I settled into the bathroom for some quality time after a busy day. Emerging relaxed, I grabbed a cold drink and headed toward the deck to sit outside and enjoy a little bird watching and all of the alcoholic content of my beverage.

As I approached the deck I noticed something odd -- a clear and unimpeded view of the backyard and lake beyond it. I realized the sliding screen was over to the left and not in its usual position at the entrance. This meant I'd left the house wide open to the elements, which I quickly became aware of when a horse fly (so named because this one was the size of a pony) started to buzz my head. I managed to shoo the beast outside as I stepped on the deck -- where I was now greeted by our cat Nate. He was outside and gave me the briefest of glances before dashing down the steps and into the yard.

Crap! I started after him but then started to think like a cat would... After a few minutes of licking my palms and rubbing my face with them, I decided to cut back through the house so I could approach Nate from the other direction and achieve the near-impossible feat of actually herding a cat toward a given destination. Amazingly, I succeeded in chasing Nate back up the steps and quickly opening the sliding screen so he could scamper in; I followed him and closed the screen behind me.

While I realize some of you with any cat-owning experience reading this may be impressed with my feline-like cunning, a few sharp-eyed folks may recall I mentioned "cats" up top. This means there was one more to be located, our orange and white fur ball Miles. I hadn't seen Miles outside with Nate, so my initial search was of all his usual indoor hiding places -- underneath the couches, behind the dryer, inside any of the floor-level cabinets (we often find him either nesting in one of the larger mixing bowls or scrunched within the blue recycling bin under the sink). He was nowhere to be found, so I went back outside and widened the search perimeter.

I checked along the boundary next to the marshy area -- no sign. I walked toward the wooden storage shed, where he'd once hidden underneath after his only prior escape from the house when we first moved in -- but he wasn't there, either. I walked the length of the driveway and didn't spot him. I then got in the car and slowly drove around our small community, looking left and right while calling his name. I did not see or hear him at all.

I returned feeling very upset with myself for not paying attention to the open doorway and permitting him to escape. Carol called at that moment to say she was leaving work and would be home after stopping to run an errand on the way. I advised her to drive slowly once she reached the house since Miles was on the loose and I didn't want him to be accidentally run over if he dashed out to greet her. Carol said she'd skip her errand and instead come straight home to join in the search effort. Once she arrived we scoured all corners of the yard and surrounding property again, then re-checked all his preferred indoor spots. Afterwards, Carol got back into her car and made another neighborhood sweep. Still no sign of our buddy.

I sunk into the couch, feeling morose and fearing for Miles's fate. He'd had a tough start to his life -- he was found on the street as a kitten, and some kind people took him in. They, however, decided they weren't really "cat people," so he ended up being adopted by some friends of our son, Josh. He would cat-sit when the friends went out of town, and after one long trip the friends returned and asked if Josh just wanted to take Miles as his own. Josh readily agreed and served as Miles's foster dad for a few years... until Josh moved to a new apartment and asked us to "temporarily" keep Miles until he got settled in. That was eight years ago. Miles moved with us from Boston to Cambridge to Dorchester and finally up to Maine. He did so along with our four OTHER cats -- Nate (short for "Concatenate" for any spreadsheet nerds out there), Sammy (Nate's brother and the sweetest cat who ever lived), Sophie and Chloe (who were unrelated strays who showed up together on our front porch one day and eventually were lured into the household). We came to Maine two years ago with all five kitties relocating with us. But those numbers have lessened over time: Chloe came down with some undetermined illness that was resistant to all treatment; Sammy developed a tumor that grew very rapidly and caused him great discomfort before we decided to put him down; and then one Friday just a few months ago we took Sophie to the vet for what we thought might have been lethargy caused by a mild infection, but two hours later were presented with a diagnosis of lymphocytic leukemia and the vet's recommendation to prevent any further inevitable decline and suffering by euthanizing her. So now we are down to just two cats -- and one was missing.

Before it got dark I said I'd take one more ride around the neighborhood to look for Miles, and Carol offered to come along. We went out onto the main road for a bit, then doubled back and slowly passed through all the ins and outs of our neighborhood. We saw no sign of Miles and no creature responded to our plaintive cries of his name. We turned into our driveway and as we came down the hill I said aloud, "We will never see him again." I pulled up next to Carol's car; I turned off the ignition and we stepped out and toward the door. There, on the other side of the glass, inside the house, sat Miles. He looked at us like, "Where ya' been?" That little fuc... er, I mean feline had apparently hidden away in some unknown, inaccessible-to-humans spot and after ninety or so minutes decided to emerge to investigate the evening's dinner offering. I was so relieved to see him I burst into tears. We ran into the house and I scooped him up in my arms, giving him a big snuggle and kiss on the head which he tolerated quite well up until the last few seconds.

I am now reminded to always check the position of the sliding screen by the memory of the near-escape, along with the reality of two large puncture wounds on my left forearm.

<u>Scalene the Heights, or Discussing Concurrent Events</u>

I recently flew to Raleigh, NC to visit with my life-long best friend, Bert. We've known each other since our junior high days, and even though it's been decades since we've lived anywhere near each other, we still manage to get together a few times each year. With all the recent fracases (fricassées?) involving airline employees and passengers, I boarded my flight with trepidation. There nearly was a moment of crisis during the first leg of my journey, when I was prepared to challenge an attendant over the fact that my snack packet contained a mere eight peanuts, one of which was rotten -- but I thought better of instigating that confrontation, deciding instead to redirect my vexation toward something positive by attempting to extricate every molecule of the minuscule amount of Diet Coke indifferently dribbled into my plastic cup full of ice.

This most recent visit was the first time since Bert started to date, and then go on to marry, his wife Marsha that just "the boys" spent a few days together. Bert's wife Marsha was visiting with family out of state, so since flights were cheaper mid-week, and Bert and I both enjoy the flexible schedules that come along with retirement, I took advantage of the lower fare while my wife Carol, who is still working, diligently earned the income necessary to subsidize my ticket.

Bert and I did what we normally do together: play tennis, jaw about politics and world events, grill a few steaks, and drink some beer. I must say -- during this visit we drank a LOT of beer. Raleigh is home to a number of craft breweries and beer-centric venues; we stopped in a number of them. But don't be alarmed -- we did not drink and drive. Well, we did not drive *very far*.

Over a couple of pints at one spot, we reminisced about the one math class we were in together, 9th-grade Geometry with Mr. Schaefer. Mr. Schaefer was an excellent teacher; very matter of fact, expert in the subject, presenting the fundamental concepts and formulas with clarity and precision. Yet, during our first grading period, we noticed he was not infallible; on occasion he'd stop mid-presentation to say, "I'm sorry, I made a mistake." He'd correct it and move on. We, however, decided to keep score, penciling tic marks inside the front covers of our textbooks each time our teacher misspoke. As the months went by, tracking of the erroneous statements piled up in neat groups of fives, and it became a race to see if Mr. Schaefer would reach the century mark before the end of the academic year.

By early May the count had reached ninety-five, so Bert and I focused less on special quadrilaterals and more on ensuring we were prepared to strike when and if the milestone occurred. Finally, with only a week remaining before the end of school, Mr. Schaefer stumbled for that hundredth time. Bert and I exchanged knowing glances but, since Mr. Schaefer seemed to be in an uncharacteristically foul mood that day, we wordlessly decided to hold off making our recognition public right then. A few days later, restored to his usual level of calm, he tripped up again and offered his usual apology. This time we were ready to spring into action. He'd made the most recent error while at the chalkboard, with his back to the class, so I interrupted him -- "Excuse me, Mr. Schaefer?" He turned around from the linear equation he was graphing and scanned the class for the source of the questioning voice. Bert and I rose from our desks and strolled confidently to the front of the room. I announced, "The two of us have been keeping count during class, and we would like to recognize you on the occasion of the one-hundredth mistake you made this year." Bert added, "Here is a certificate we commissioned to document this historic occasion." He presented Mr. Schaefer with something we'd lettered on a piece of blank paper, with a ribbon affixed to it; we each grabbed his free hand to shake it; we returned to our seats.

Mr. Schaefer stood speechless for some time, shaking his head, glancing again at the certificate, then squinting toward the two perpetrators. Eventually, he managed to stammer, "Thank you... I think," before placing the award on his desk and returning to the formula he was showing us how to solve. Shortly thereafter the bell rang, and we filed out of class.

I don't believe anyone other than Bert and myself found what we'd done amusing or entertaining in the least -- none of our classmates, and certainly not Mr. Schaefer. But that didn't matter; WE thought it was hilarious. We'd spent the better part of a year focused on a mission requiring attention to detail and meticulous planning -- with a modicum of math, via the tic marks -- all of which served to reinforce our standing as friends. Even as the transitions to high school, then college, then careers and relationships have taken us in different directions, we've always maintained that closeness -- for over forty years at this point.

We're quite a contrast of opposites. Bert is tall and slender; I'm short and stocky. He's mechanically inclined and can repair or rebuild nearly anything; I'm intimidated by power tools and take at least two tries to successfully change the batteries in a flashlight. His groundstrokes are elegant; I'm all about the big serve. And yet we have this connection -- stronger, I think, than between many brothers. I'm sure it's no coincidence we're both only children. (By that, I mean neither of us has any siblings, not that we're emotionally immature -- at least, Bert isn't.)

Bert made excellent use of his facility with mathematics, becoming a successful, well-regarded civil/structural engineer. I used my math skills to calculate what I was sacrificing by leaving several jobs before becoming fully vested in their retirement plans, eventually landing at a company where I was rapidly promoted, becoming progressively less effective in each new role, and finally securing a position in middle management where I reached my level of incompetence before being laid off.

That's all behind us now. More tennis, more steaks, and more beer await. I believe we learned a formula in that long-ago class that would permit me to graph the changes in velocity of my devastating serve as it explodes from my racquet, caroms off the deuce court, and bounces just beyond Bert's flailing reach. But all I really remember from Geometry is that damn certificate.

Section 2: Clutch Performance

Hush Little Baby

I came downstairs the other morning to find a pile of laundry at the foot of the steps. Not washed and folded laundry neatly placed in a basket and ready to carry upstairs -- but a pile of disheveled clothes that needed to be relocated about twelve feet WNW in front of the washing machine. I made a necessary but perhaps slightly exaggerated stride to step over the clutter and enter the kitchen. Carol looked in my direction; I nodded my head toward the mess on the floor and quizzically raised my eyebrows. "Oh, shut up..." she replied.

I think it's unfair for someone to call you out for thoughts not yet expressed; don't you? I mean, sure -- I *may* have been forming a coherent sentence questioning why the laundry had been left in that spot, but I also may have been giving consideration to extraneous factors and found myself willing to come down on the side of good intentions gone awry. This would be the difference between asking, "Why did you dump the laundry at the foot of the stairs?" and "I suppose you think you had a good reason for dumping the laundry at the foot of the stairs?" It's all in the context.

It turned out one of the cats cut across Carol's path as she came off that last step, so she dropped the clothes to grab the railing and keep from tripping. Fair enough -- but I was still puzzled as to why the pile remained there afterward, creating a hazard for other household members to avoid. Such as myself. Over the next few minutes, I kept one eye on the pile and the other on Carol as she fixed breakfast for us before getting herself ready for work, making myself a little wall-eyed since she never approached the mess to complete its delivery to the laundry area. Finally, I decided to take charge, scooping up the clothes and placing them in front of the washing machine. As soon as I did so, Carol called out to me: "As long as you're going to do laundry, would you also throw my yoga clothes in? And remember they do NOT go in the dryer -- you have to hang them up." Before I could even respond Carol added, "... and there's also a load of towels." Well, so much for *my* plans for the day.

I got through the multiple loads of laundry, shrinking only a couple pairs of Carol's yoga pants -- a solid 4 out of 5 for effort. I also put together a vegetarian dinner that neither one of us was all that interested in eating, but at least it's now sitting in the fridge if we feel a need to partake of something "healthy" later in the week. I vacuumed, brushed the cats, vacuumed again and thought long and hard about mopping the kitchen floor, ultimately deciding against it since I didn't care to exude the aroma of Pine-Sol for the rest of the day.

When Carol came home that evening, she checked on the laundry and expressed her dismay about the yoga pants that were now better suited for a toddler to wear. I considered putting a positive spin on it, referencing my 80% success rate with the remaining clothing and also mentioning that if she felt she could do a better job she was welcome to handle the task her own self, and also had she noticed how nice the carpet looked after being vacuumed other than the swath under the dining room table where much of the cat hair had collected -- but I decided against giving her so much to sort through at one time.

That would just be piling it on.

Death Fakes a Holiday

Some years back, as we were watching TV one evening, my wife's ears suddenly pricked up and she leapt from the couch. "What's the matter?" I asked. "It's Josh," she replied. "He's crying." Apparently, he was howling at a frequency only a mother could hear.

Carol dashed upstairs, returning several minutes later with the nine-year-old Josh trailing behind, his face flushed, eyes wet and using his pajama sleeve to wipe his tears and runny nose. Carol informed me Josh was upset about something and wanted to discuss it with both of us.

"What's the matter, buddy?" I asked, extending my arms and offering him a reassuring smile while trying to keep one eye on the courtroom histrionics unfolding during the second half of *Law & Order*. We discussed a concern common among children around his age -- he had begun to wrestle with the concept of mortality.

Josh told us how he realized his grandparents were getting older and one day "soon" they would die, as would his parents and friends and pets. There was no reference to his own eventual demise but I chose not to press him on that omission.

His mother and I took turns consoling him, trying to respond truthfully without introducing undue alarm. We trotted out all the usual homilies -- death is a part of life, everybody/everything dies, it's not going to happen for a long time, yes we had named him as our sole beneficiary, etc. He eventually calmed down, seemingly placated by our reassurances, and soon went back to bed.

A few nights later, just as the late news came on, we heard footsteps and Josh came around the corner into the living room. Again he had been crying and was distraught. "What's wrong, honey?" his mother asked. He stopped sobbing long enough to exclaim, "It's <u>death</u> again!" We pulled him onto the couch between us and had a conversation very similar to the previous one. In between sniffles he said his latest worry was around whether we were going to establish a living trust so he could avoid probate. I offered him a tissue and while he blew his nose I said we'd certainly give it some thought.

The subject eventually faded from discussion and the only other time after that I recall hearing Josh cry out in the middle of the night was about a year later. Carol and I dashed through the dark into his room to ask what was wrong. He was terrified because "There's a spider trying to kill me!" We said that was ridiculous and turned on the light so we could show him it was just his imagination. After flipping the switch, we saw a spider the size of a silver dollar descending from the ceiling light fixture along a thin line of silk, hovering inches from his face. It was a scene right out of a horror film and all that was missing was a girlish high-pitched shriek, which I obligingly provided. Carol, keeping her wits, ran to grab some toilet paper and quickly wrapped up the beast, relocating it to the commode and a swirling end of days. None of us, most importantly Josh, seemed upset in the least by how abruptly the spider had been forced to confront its mortality, and our son fell back asleep before inquiring as to the disposition of the arachnid's estate.

I thought of these vignettes after reading an article in our local newspaper about the sudden death of a man after shoveling snow. To clarify these events: both the man and I had recently shoveled snow; after that the man died, and after that I read about it. In the past when I'd heard about such tragedies I didn't pay much attention since the decedent was usually someone well into middle age, older than me. But this time I noticed the man was age 54; I'd just turned 59. This gave me pause; I thought about my own mortality along with what I could do to make sure I didn't succumb to a similar fate from future attempts at this specific endeavor. I read an article about proper body mechanics when shoveling snow, reminders to pace oneself when doing so, and also considered whether it made sense to acquire a snow blower to lessen my exertion. I love to get a new toy as much as the next guy, but decent snow blowers are expensive -- so I weighed my available options and return on investment while factoring in my blood pressure and cholesterol levels. After calculating the probabilities, I implemented the most effective course of action to all but guarantee I would never meet my demise as a result of shoveling snow: I make Carol do it now.

The Midnight Rile We All Must Hear

Listen, dear voters, and you shall hear
Of the kinds of surprises politicos fear.
In the month of October, Two-Zero-Sixteen
Hardly any evidence remained still unseen.
Who can forget that famous video?

One candidate said to his friend, "I'm a star!
I'm rich! And they've all seen me on the TV.
I really just don't care who most of them are --
I put out my hand and I grab their p***y.
One if by jet, and two if by bus
There's more than enough chicks for the two of us.
Ready to grab and cause great alarm.
I want them for sex; they'll succumb to my charm.
When that fails, then Tic-Tacs I use to disarm."

He sort of apologized – then with hair a-flutter
Returned to the trail, launching yet more attacks.
But all of a sudden one more, then another
Made claims that, in years past, consent he had lacked.
He said, "All are liars! I never molested!
I'll sue! I will win once my case has been rested."
The clamor distracted from what John Podesta'd
Allegedly said, since his emails were hacked.

Meanwhile, his opponent, through every device
Sent emails without confidentiality.
Totally disregarding sage advice,
And claimed to not know the meaning of "C."
First she denied it, then she proclaimed
In hindsight she should have accepted some blame.
Yet nothing was criminal – Comey said the same.
But just when we thought a review had been thorough
A new warning came from the Federal Bureau.

While following up on the trail of a sexter
Who shared a device with her closest aide,
The FBI found more emails sure to vex her.
This scandal was one that would not go away.
No sooner would Hillary claim, "All is well!"
Then some revelation would bring a fresh hell.
Over and over, it was a tough sell.
She'd battled; established a lead with the electorate
But doubts of her trustworthiness may have wrecked it.

On through the campaign trudge Hillary and Donald
With near every night yet another reveal.
Claims from yet one more woman he fondled;
Money her foundation may have concealed.
A voice in the darkness, a knock at the door,
His claim if she wins – Second Amendment no more.
She says he's unqualified, dangerous to boot.
If he wins, she says our society will uproot.
In this hour of darkness and peril and need
The people will waken and wish they could hear
A message of hope, an inspiring creed.
Instead of this campaign that generates fear.
We want inspiration – we get rant and rave.
While patriot Paul Revere spins in his grave.

Clutter Nonsense

I straightened up in the bathroom the other day and placed a clean throw rug in front of the sink. When Carol came home that evening, she saw the rug and told me: "I don't want that on the floor." My response: "Where else would it go?"

I knew she meant she didn't want that particular rug on display, but I have so few opportunities to zing her that I had to jump on the non-sequitur. More importantly -- why, then, were we holding onto something we no longer had any use for? We recently bought another storage shed to join the one we already have in the yard; the new one serves as a place for all the furniture we continue to keep that does not fit into our current home. When we moved to our lovely but modest lake house in Maine, instead of downsizing our possessions, we brought everything with us and just gerrymandered the boundaries within which they are legally permitted to reside.

When company comes, we offer a comfortable guest room with a few tastefully arranged family heirlooms on display. However, we're able to do that only by relocating an insane amount of stuff into our bedroom for the duration of their stay -- several barrels' worth of family photographs and craft supplies, stacks of books and magazines, assorted folding chairs, two sewing machines, and my exercise bicycle (which is actually a full-sized bike with the rear wheel sitting on a training stand so I can peddle furiously without actually going anywhere, much like when I ride the bike outside). We can't show overnight visitors the master bedroom on the house tour since we have to put a shoulder to our door to force it open.

Once in a great while when we are house cleaning (and by this, I mean that we house clean only once in a great while), Carol will look at me and say, "I'm in a mood to get rid of things." This is a rare event, like a visit from Halley's Comet, or a truthful statement under oath from a member of the Trump administration. We immediately jump into action once those words leave her lips; we fill box after box with no-longer-worn clothing, no-longer-used kitchen appliances, no-longer-functioning electronic devices and other redundant possessions, and rush them to Goodwill before regret has time to take hold. We unload so much during these trips that the IRS dispatches an agent to supervise the donations. Once everything is accounted for, we receive a completed Form 8283 for "Noncash Charitable Contributions," and to express our thanks we offer a bottle of wine (valued at $20 or less, as per federal guidelines), throwing in a few sticker books if the agent happens to mention there are small children at home.

Some people find it hard to give up things they rarely (if ever) use because of emotional connections to those items. That extra set of china that's sitting in a box up in the attic? It belonged to your grandparents. That collection of Instamatic cameras, which they don't make film for anymore? You've held on to them since adolescence, when your life's ambition was to become a photographer for National Geographic. The dress you wore to your senior prom? That's the night you lost your... contact lenses. These keepsakes remind you of connections to family, or special events, or a time when your vision of the future excited you more than it might right now. I tend to be less sentimental than my wife, so it often falls on me in these moments to remain objective and ask that perfectly rational question: "Why do you want to hold onto something you no longer have any use for?"

Lately, I notice Carol staring at me for a long, long time before answering.

Eques-tryin'

Horses are pessimists. I guess they can't help it since they're all born neigh-sayers.

I asked for a pony for Christmas and found a 7-ounce bottle of beer under the tree. It took the edge off my disappointment.

It's inadvisable to saddle a horse with your problems. Makes for a rough ride.

Likewise, you should avoid trying to stirrup trouble, unless "Trouble" is your horse's name.

Someone asked me if I was interested in horse racing. I said of course not; certainly the horse was going to beat me every time.

A horse's teeth take up a larger amount of space in their head than their brain. Same with Donald Trump.

As many times as I've heard someone use the phrase, "She was rode hard and put away wet" -- it was never in reference to a horse.

Did you know horses love to sing? That's why you find them in a chorale.

A Jewish horse who loves to sing is called a "canter".

Horses don't believe in the institution of marriage. That's why you never see them included in a bridle party.

Every time I ask to borrow $10 from a younger horse, he says he has nothing to lend. I suppose that's because a foal and his money are soon parted.

Someone who shoes horses is called a farrier. If he overcharges for the service, he's called an unfarrier.

I've got spurs that jingle, jangle, jingle. For that I was referred to an orthopedist.

I went to see a horseplay once. It was *Othello*, with the lead role played by a dark horse.

Wild horses couldn't drag me away. But my wife's hairdryer trips the bathroom circuit and suddenly I'm expected to jump up from the couch.

Getting Out Of (not out in) Nature

I rarely approach topics from a serious perspective, yet there are times I feel the need to make an exception. This is not one of them.

Camping is a complete waste of time, and here are my reasons:

Why do people say they want to get closer to nature and then separate themselves from it by erecting a nylon barrier?

It's a popular family activity which everyone seems to enjoy except for the parents and their children. "Let's take our rambunctious crew of hyperactive adolescents, ages 3, 5, 7 and 10 -- plus the baby and dog -- remove them from an environment where all that is needed to fulfill their daily demands is conveniently at hand, and relocate them to a distant locale where every single necessity of daily life presents a logistical challenge and is therefore often forsworn. Also the inevitable rain."

When I want to "get away from it all," I go out for a beer like normal people.

Think about it -- why would you want to sleep on a lumpy surface inside a poorly ventilated enclosure where the smell of other people's farts (not to mention your own) has no path of escape?

People talk about mitigating the risks inherent with camping -- keeping food safe from bears, skin safe from insects, possessions safe from interlopers. There's a foolproof method to accomplish all of this, called "staying home."

Many folks share a romantic vision of being in the Great Outdoors: a day filled with strenuous, invigorating activity; evenings filled with hearty, flame-grilled meals followed by a restful night's sleep on a bedroll in the open air under a vast expanse of star-filled sky while listening to the distant cries of native wildlife. Kind of like the first twenty minutes of *Brokeback Mountain*, but then it went off in a different direction.

When I was younger, I would regularly carry essential supplies and my own meals into an environment filled with the unknown; where the only way to get to my next destination was to walk along unfamiliar pathways; where I would often arrive not properly prepared for the weather or other challenges I was about to face; where I would surrender my need for order and control to the direction of a higher authority; where even though there may have been others around me I often felt truly alone. This was called "high school" and I don't care to repeat the experience.

My few and far-between camping experiences include these highlights: a bear trashing our cooler; a chipped tooth from trying to inflate an air mattress without a pump; a cold front moving in overnight, bringing temperatures below freezing in late August; a late-night dash out of the tent to pee aborted by an encounter with the aforementioned bear, and someone serving me decaf one morning without notice, resulting in a withdrawal headache so severe that it was all I could do to spend ten uninterrupted minutes cursing out the person who handed me the cup.

Now when I feel the urge to camp, I take a leisurely walk through the nearest Cabela's while examining the gear and stuffed critters. Once I've had my fill of the Great Indoors, I buy a piece of fudge, exhale contentedly and drive home. And before I hit the road -- they also provide a safe place to pee.

Road Hard, Put Away Wet

Virtually every little boy and girl (and, in the spirit of inclusiveness, every gender-fluid child) in our country dreams of growing up and becoming President one day. I have a message for the youngsters of our nation: it can happen for you -- because it happened to me.

Last Saturday, I was elected President. Granted, it was as the head of our local road association, but still... The title is "President" and I accepted the honor with grace and humility. That morning we held our annual association meeting; the vote in favor of my candidacy was unanimous. I suspect this is less a reflection of my popularity among my neighbors and more that no one else was remotely interested in the job. Nonetheless, it will make a nice accomplishment for my future biographer to highlight.

A neighbor down the street served as President for the last two years, but this year decided she was ~~fed up had~~ other interests to pursue and so declined another term in office. She called me a few weeks ago to ask if I would consider running for the job (I believe the actual request was: "Are you willing to do it? Because I sure as shit can't be bothered anymore."); if so, she would place my name in nomination. As flattered as I was, I still approached the opportunity with a level head and had a few questions for her:

- How much is the presidential stipend?
- Why is there no presidential stipend?
- Does the President have check-signing authority?
- Have the association's accounts ever been audited?

Once I felt I had a grasp of the position's parameters, I went about assembling my campaign team and preparing a press release announcing my candidacy. Much to my surprise, the so-called Mainstream Media had zero interest in covering the news. No reporters attended the rally I staged in my backyard, which meant I'd thrown two packs of hot dogs on the grill for naught. Come to think of it, I don't recall seeing any of my neighbors there, either. Our local ad-supported weekly publication said for a small fee they'd run a short write-up, so I emailed them the

42

release. I was excited when I saw the article in print but was very disappointed when both my first and last names were misspelled. I contacted the editor, who told me that proofing cost extra. Sigh... Well, this was not a disaster on the level of Muskie bursting into tears back in '72 (which seems so quaint compared to what we witnessed in 2016, yes?), so I shook up the team (which, so far, was only my wife and myself -- and one of us had to go. Sorry, honey...) and pressed on.

I won't draw any comparisons between the 2016 campaign and my own, with this exception -- say what you want about the two major candidates and the election outcome, but regardless of party affiliation many folks say one flaw in Hillary's effort was that she came across as distant and remote, not embracing the kind of hands-on "retail politics" her husband Bill was famous for. I did not want to repeat that mistake, so I launched a walking tour to make the acquaintance of as many of my potential constituents as possible. There are only twenty houses on our road, and half of them aren't owner-occupied year-round, but that did not deter me from knocking on every door in an effort to hear from the community and present my case. I didn't take it personally when a few folks slammed their doors in my face, or when I clearly saw people through the screen sitting in their living rooms yet resolutely ignoring my "Hello!" -- but the third time someone sicced their dog on me, I decided my time was better spent disseminating my platform via social media.

Using several popular online platforms, I got an honest, unfiltered message out to my future subjects neighbors. They weren't much for the Twitter, but I did get quite a few comments in response to my Facebook posts. However, they were mostly links to cat videos or pictures of their grandchildren. A couple of them were videos of their grandchildren playing with cats.

I woke up early the morning of the association meeting and rehearsed my stump speech. As an effort to get out the vote, I brought travel-sized bottles of Maalox and Kaopectate to distribute. But, as I mentioned above, nearly all the preparation was rendered unnecessary since no opponent emerged to challenge me. Nonetheless, I was proud of the campaign I'd run: focused on the issues (well, just the one issue -- overseeing maintenance of the road), no negative messaging (instead of accusing anyone of exceeding the posted 15 MPH speed limit, I thanked everyone who honored the voluntary 8:30 PM curfew), with appeal to a broad demographic, which in this case was men and women, mostly retired, ages 60 to 85.

Now that the election is behind me -- the focus is on a future of leading with clear vision and a steady hand. Both of which will be necessary since I've just learned the Association's finances are in the red, so apparently I'm expected to use my snow blower to clear everyone's driveway this winter and also operate a grader to re-level the road once we get through next spring's mud season. My advice to those dreaming youngsters? Take your time, do your research, and make sure you understand the span of responsibilities you'll be expected to embrace. It would be devastating, in response to your decision to chase elective office, to have people accuse you of Russian into it.

Off the Rack or Why the Dishwasher Isn't Emptied

You asked me what I had to do that was so important I couldn't empty the dishwasher. Here is that list:

Finish the taxes. They're due the day after... Dammit! Doesn't <u>anyone</u> ever change the wall calendar at the end of the month?

Head over to the hardware store and pick up the box of screws I need to reattach the ceiling fan to the fixture. You told me if you tripped over that fan on the carpet one more time you didn't know WHAT you would do. I, however, have a pretty good idea. Yes, I know the exact size I need... yay-long (holding up thumb and forefinger to illustrate).

Trim the hedges before it's necessary to rent a bucket lift.

Check the rodent traps in the crawlspace under the house. Which I will do as soon as I can find my boots, coveralls, leather gloves and safety goggles. Do you have a hairnet I can borrow? Never mind, I'll use your shower cap.

Get my Kickstarter campaign going. No, I think there are <u>plenty</u> of people who would be willing to purchase a mattress with a built-in disposable sheet dispenser.

Change the oil in your car. Oh, wait -- we're still using the ramps until I fix the front steps.

Download that app you said uses games to improve memory. What's it called again? And have you seen my phone?

Change the batteries in the smoke detectors. If you weren't always after me to do one damn thing after another around here, I would have changed them months ago and now we wouldn't have those scorch marks on the kitchen ceiling, would we?

Repaint the kitchen ceiling.

Pick up the two quarts of native strawberries you asked me to get for that pie you're planning to take over to our neighbor who is recuperating from her hospital stay. Oh, I'm sorry... when was the funeral?

Continue training for the 10k that's coming up in another few... Dammit! Doesn't <u>anyone</u> ever change the wall calendar at the end of the month?

Backup all our files to that new external hard drive our son gave us last Christmas. I'll take care of it as soon as I can figure out why the computer display isn't coming on.

Remember to tell you the dishwasher is broken.

Section 3: Them's The Brakes

Thirteen Last-Minute Gift Ideas for Your Holidays

As I write this, Christmas, Hanukkah, and Kwanzaa are still more than two weeks away and yet all the "hot" holiday gift items seem to be in short supply. When you call the Snuggies people and are told the only choice left is the Two-Tone in Gold and Avocado Chevron Stripes, size 3XL.... It's time to get creative so as not to completely stiff the people upon whom you are counting to give you much nicer gifts than you reluctantly purchased for them.

Here are thirteen gift ideas for those of you who have waited too long and/or were hoping for a Bernie Sanders victory and his subsequent issuance of an ushanka to every citizen of the New Socialist Republic to celebrate the secular Winter Solstice:

1. **Donald Trump Gift Basket of Deplorable Foods:** A delectable assortment of fried chicken, french fries, and overcooked steaks, but absolutely no humble pie.

2. **Mike Pence Stopwatch:** Click on the timer and watch it run backward to a simpler time when men (real men, if you catch my drift) knew what was best for everyone else.

3. **Hillary Clinton Glass Ceiling Cleaner:** May not perform as expected in shattering your expectations.

4. **Tim Kaine Vanishing Cream:** Apply and watch yourself disappear back into obscurity.

5. **Jill Stein Abacus:** However you do the math, it still doesn't add up. (Also available in Pat McCrory Special Edition.)

6. **Gary Johnson Compass:** No matter where you are, you'll still be directionless.

7. **GOP Candy Sampler:** 17 assorted varieties, mostly nuts, a few clusterfucks, some milquetoast with only one dark to choose

from, and one with a surprisingly bitter finish after all the rest have been consumed and cast aside.

8. **DNC Vanity Mirror:** Originally designed to reflect a bright future but unexpectedly shatters in the harsh morning-after dawn of reality.

9. **The 2016 Ford "Millennial":** Doesn't burn expensive fossil fuels because it's not going anywhere. Special 100% self-interest financing available.

10. **Rainbow Coalition Flag:** Sorry, now available only in White.

11. **Vegetable Repealer:** Puts things back the way they were before, regardless of how beneficial they were once offered for your consumption.

12. **Alt-Right Guard Deodorant:** Covers up the stench but there's still a festering reality causing the stink that you ignore at your own peril.

13. **Fake News of the World Subscription (online edition):** All the post-truth, fact-free, false-flag, conspiracy-obsessed stories that stubbornly refuse to go away. Free pizza with every order!

--

Please make your checks payable to "My Non-Existent Charitable Foundation" to make your purchase tax-avoidable. Delivery by Christmas is, according to the mainstream media, all but guaranteed. If you are not satisfied with your purchase, you can tweet about it but at your own peril.

In the face of some truly ridiculous legislation recently steamrollered into existence by so-called "leadership" in the states of North Carolina and Mississippi -- and here I'm referring actions far more significant than the governors of both states signing proclamations declaring April as "Safe Digging Month" (really) -- allow me to recall a few of my most awkward attempts over the years to express support for the LGBTQ community.

Early in my career, I worked as a customer service agent for a large telecommunications company. During periods of sparse call volume, we'd handle correspondence, opening and reading letters (this is back when people still put pen to paper) and shuttling them to the appropriate department to prepare a reply. During one shift I handled a letter from someone who expressed his dismay that my employer was hostile to gay employees. Seeking guidance where to direct this missive I showed it to my supervisor, feeling for some reason I should add my own amused observation that this person was misinformed since "we have gay folks all over this place." I meant this in an inclusive, not invasive, way but that distinction did not register with my boss. In my own mind, I was attempting to express favorable recognition that I was part of a diverse workplace; this job was my first exposure -- so far as I knew -- to openly gay people in a professional setting (back when being closeted was much more the rule than the exception). What I did not know was that the company had not always treated its gay employees fairly, and this letter was part of a social action campaign supporting a lawsuit intended to eliminate institutionalized discrimination. What I also did not know was that my supervisor was gay. I'm sure my comment sounded to him just like those made by so many others trying to hide prejudice behind self-immunizing statements, such as, "Some of my best friends are [insert marginalized population]." He shot a stern glance in my direction, provided a quick history lesson regarding the underlying legal issue, and provided instruction for the proper next steps to make sure the protest was correctly registered and responded to. I was beyond embarrassed and, after filing the letter, gave serious thought to how I could better express my open-mindedness regarding sexual orientation and gender identity. I also decided to no longer rely on my obviously defective gaydar.

Decades later I was working for a company that had signed an amicus brief in support of the (eventually successful) effort to overturn the Defense of Marriage Act. This company consistently and enthusiastically supported the advancement of gay rights as part of the corporate culture. During a visit to one of our field offices, the area director took me out to lunch. For most of the meal we talked only business, but after ordering coffee the director shifted the conversation to inquire about my family status. I answered and then asked the same question in return since he had broached the subject. His reply: "Well, I have a rather unconventional lifestyle. I live with my partner and we are raising an 18-month-old." The only things about this arrangement that initially struck me as "unconventional" were that he didn't specify the gender of the toddler or pull up any baby pictures on his phone. Or perhaps they had acquired an orphaned tiger cub, or were really into nurturing some sort of exotic house plant? With his mention of "unconventional lifestyle" and "partner" in such close proximity I made an assumption -- one intended to come from a place of acceptance -- and decided to launch into an illustrative anecdote to express my understanding of his situation. A summary here: a man I once offered a job to said he couldn't start work for another month because he'd gotten married a year ago and had anniversary travel plans. I offered my congratulations, asking what the couple was planning to do. He said they were going to Ireland and the trip was centered around playing golf together. I was about to say, "How nice that you and your wife both enjoy golfing," but just before speaking out loud a little bell went off in my head and I said "spouse" rather than "wife." This was a good thing since he then confirmed what an avid golfer his husband was. I related this story to my lunch companion to send a clear signal that I was "cool" with the concept of same-sex unions. There was an unexpected silence before the director looked me in the eye and said, "My partner is a woman. We have a child together but aren't married; that's the unconventional part. I'm not gay."

"Oh, that wasn't my point at all!" I quickly scrambled. "I only meant to convey my feeling that as long as two people love and respect each other there's no reason to think of their relationship as 'unconventional'." I think in the history of CYA attempts this one should have received an award.

These days I'm glad to have among our friends those who have chosen to share their sexual identities with us as well those who haven't -- gay, straight or somewhere in-between, it doesn't matter and quite frankly is none of our damn business. Nor should it be the government's. Why can't we proclaim it's safe to dig that?

<u>Climb Every Mantra</u>

Carol asked me the other day if I'd be interested in going to Kol Nidre with her that evening. I was confused by her request, since: 1) it wasn't anywhere near Yom Kippur, and 2) Carol isn't Jewish. When I asked her to clarify the reason behind her inquiry, she said it would help us learn to focus and relax. Now I was completely flummoxed, so I turned off the TV, pulled out my earphones, stopped scrolling through Facebook on my phone and stepped down from the treadmill. "*What* exactly is it you want to do tonight?"

Once I was paying closer attention I understood she was asking if I wanted to practice *Yoga Nidra* with her. Ah, OK -- to the untrained ear, Aramaic and Sanskrit sound an awful lot alike. I was forced to admit I knew as much about Yoga Nidra as Carol knew about Kol Nidre, so I asked her to provide a brief explanation. She said it was a method of achieving deep relaxation; getting the mind and body into a state of consciousness between waking and sleeping. I said I wasn't sure why this was something that required practice since that's how I spend most of my days. She went on to clarify that the focus was more on achieving a "wakeful" state while still being very relaxed, and when one reaches such a condition the body rejuvenates and the mind opens to profound insights. I said I wasn't sure this was all that different from attending Yom Kippur services, which also cultivated drowsiness while requiring you to remain attentive. Carol said the two were nothing alike and suggested once the Yoga Nidra session was done we could go out to eat. I said she was further proving my point; the highlight of the Day of Atonement is the meal when it's all over. But because I am open to new experiences and also because Carol gave me "that look" -- I agreed to go with her.

After we arrived at the yoga studio, I had to sign a release. "Release from what?" was my question; I had to agree I wouldn't hold the business liable for any injury that might occur during the session. I asked what kind of injury could possibly be inflicted while trying to achieve a state of deep relaxation while stretched out prone on a mat at floor level, unless I somehow managed to be lulled into an irreversible coma? Again, Carol gave me "that look;" I acquiesced and signed the paperwork. We ditched our shoes and I dropped my attitude.

This was a popular program; there must have been at least sixty people in the room. I wondered how anyone could achieve a state of deep relaxation in such a crowded, enclosed space. I thought perhaps the tight quarters combined with deep breathing would lead to elevated levels of CO_2, and therefore people were confusing profound insights with hallucinations brought on by oxygen deprivation. Now I was understanding why I had to sign that release.

The session got underway with several basic yoga poses, focused on gentle stretching and alignment, which caused me to break into a sweat while fighting off foot cramps. About fifteen minutes in we began to work on our state of consciousness. We lay still while listening to our instructor, a very knowledgeable and charming woman named Sagel, review the seven chocolates. There are *seven* kinds of chocolate? Let's see: there's Snickers, 3 Musketeers, Twix, KitKat, Mounds, Almond Joy... I was drawing a blank on the last one. I whispered to Carol on my left to ask if she knew, and she replied we were supposed to be focusing on the seven chakras. Well, Jesus -- I could relax, or I could focus on chakras, but how could I possibly do BOTH AT THE SAME TIME?

I don't recall the specifics of the seven chakras because, in all honesty, by that point I was craving something sweet. Once we were done with the chakras, Sagel had us direct our focus on individual parts of the body: sections of the arm; the leg; the torso, head and neck... She named every appendage by name except for the tingly parts.

Next came instruction to focus on the breath flowing through each nostril, individually. I could pick the left side of my nose (I don't mean "pick" that way) but couldn't manage to isolate the right. Left-breathing is supposed to lower your blood pressure, while right-breathing raises it back up. The risk of lapsing into a coma was inching closer to reality.

Since the class had people ranging from novice to expert, Sagel said we should each do whatever we felt was necessary to relax. So... I got up and dashed into the pub next door for a quick beer. I would have slipped back into my spot unnoticed except for belching as I resumed my Savasana pose.

We completed the session after another thirty minutes. Sagel then guided our return to a "normal" state of awareness. Well, for everyone except the woman who was on my right -- she was sleeping like a baby. I kneeled down, gently putting a hand on her shoulder while leaning in close to her ear to say, "WAKE UP! IT'S OVER!!" Everyone rolled up their yoga mats, re-folded blankets, returned blocks to storage, and exuded a sense of calm and well-being. I have to admit -- I enjoyed the session more than I thought I would, finding it very peaceful. I felt more centered than when I arrived, and actually had an insight unearthed from deep in my subconscious which helped me resolve an issue that had been preying on my mind for much of the evening: the seventh chocolate is a Milky Way.

Namaste.

Double Double Toilet Trouble

Our good friends Bert and Marsha came up for a visit this past week. We were celebrating a number of special occasions -- Bert's 60th birthday; his retirement at the end of the month; our long-standing relationships, both singly and as couples.

Plans for our time together included, as always, enjoying good food, wine and beer, the resumption of a decades-long tennis rivalry between Bert and myself, and our wives getting their chakras aligned during a yoga session. After spending the weekend at our place we'd drive to Acadia National Park for a few days of sightseeing, bolstered with some shopping in the various quaint towns on Mount Desert Island. Here's the chronicle of our action-packed time together:

SATURDAY

- Carol and I leave the house fifteen minutes late for our drive to Portland to pick up Bert and Marsha, who are flying up from Raleigh.
- We return to the house to get Carol's sunglasses.
- And once again for her cell phone.
- As we speed toward the airport I wish I had taken advantage of one of those two U-turns to relieve myself.
- We arrive only to find their flight is delayed. We cool our heels in the cell phone lot, which is devoid of men's or women's rooms, for thirty minutes while waiting for our friends to summon us to the Arrivals area.
- We pick them up and start to head downtown for some lunch and exploration.
- Before we exit the airport, we pull into the cell phone lot again so Marsha can get a sweater out of her suitcase to ward off the brisk Maine fall weather.
- Shockingly, we find a parking spot right in front of the restaurant where we plan to have lunch.
- We enter and I make a beeline for the restroom before we place our order. The others follow suit.
- I return to the car to put change in the parking meter.

- I return to the car again to get Carol's jacket since it's chilly in the restaurant.
- After lunch, we stroll to a neighboring coffee shop to warm up.
- I return to the restaurant to retrieve the credit card I left behind.
- I return to the car to put more change in the parking meter.
- After finishing our coffee, we get ready to visit two local breweries to enjoy samples in their tasting rooms. But before leaving, I step into the single bathroom.
- Then Marsha does the same.
- Then Bert.
- Then Carol.
- By now, I have to go again so I visit the ~~men's~~ gender-neutral's room one more time.
- Approaching the brewery, parking is limited so we prowl for an extended period. When a tight space opens up I masterfully squeeze into it. Carol objects to having to slither out of her door but I don't hear her complaint since I am dashing inside to find the toilet.
- The others enter and immediately head for the stalls.
- We order our brews, find a table, and some of us saunter toward the W.C. again.
- After we finish our beer, Marsha goes to buy a souvenir t-shirt while the rest of us return to the privy.
- We strike out for the second brewery. Once we arrive, I tell Carol what to order for me while I look for the latrine.
- We carry our drinks to the outside patio area. I have both mine and Carol's in my hands since she has gone to the powder room.
- We finish and decamp for the car, making a quick dash back inside to use the john.
- We pull into our driveway an hour and fifteen minutes later. Before I even put it in Park, Carol jumps out of the still-moving car so she can be the first into our one and only washroom.
- That evening we make a nice home-cooked meal for our company, enjoying a few bottles of wine with dinner. Between their early departure for the airport that morning and the number of adult beverages consumed during the day, Bert and Marsha are ready to turn in early. Bert asks if anyone wants to

use the loo before he gets ready for bed, and the three of us take turns.

- Forty minutes later, Bert finally has a chance to wash up. As he exits, I barge past him in order to take care of business once more.
- We all stagger upstairs to our respective bedrooms for a good night's sleep.

SUNDAY

- I wake up at 5:15 AM with an urgent need to visit the little boy's room. I decide to stay up and get breakfast prepped. As Carol, Bert and Marsha wander downstairs later that morning, I ask everyone how they slept and the responses are startlingly similar - "Fine, except when I got up at two/three/four o'clock to pee."
- After breakfast, we take turns using the shower. Hours later, everyone is washed and dressed and now it's time for lunch.
- We drive to Hallowell so our guests can check out our favorite spot there. Great food and very spacious commodes.
- After lunch, we park at a spot down by the Kennebec River where the town has placed colorful Adirondack chairs. We sit and chat idly while looking for sturgeon, osprey, and eagles, keeping one eye on the Porta Potty and alerting each other as it becomes vacant.
- After returning home, Bert and I decide to play tennis as the ladies get ready to go to their yoga session. This necessitates everyone needing to complete their toilette.
- Bert runs me around the court like a reporter rushing to find the source of Donald Trump's fantastical claims. Remaining gracious in defeat, I permit Bert to be first to visit the head when we get back to the house.
- We spend the rest of the afternoon watching football, eating Cheez-Its, drinking beer and occasionally seeing a man about a horse.

MONDAY

- Stuffing enough luggage into the back of the car to last for a month-long ocean cruise, we leave for our two-night stay in Bar Harbor.
- As we approach town, we check the directions for our lodging and discover it's not in Bar Harbor as we thought but instead thirty minutes away in Southwest Harbor. We ask Google Maps to redirect us and also query, "Where's the closest bathroom?"
- We check into a lovely B&B where the only drawback is the steep stairway from the lobby to the second and third floors. Climbing the steps rivals using the iron rungs needed to scale Acadia's Precipice Trail.
- That evening we go out to celebrate Bert's birthday with dinner at a first-rate restaurant in Bar Harbor where the only drawback is the seven-minute walk from our table to find the doors marked "Hommes" and "Femmes" located back in the bar area.

TUESDAY

- We plan to spend our one full day in the park making several hikes. We've chosen to start with the Ocean Walk, which offers spectacular coastal views along with a marked pedestrian crossing that leads to public facilities in the parking lot across the road from famous Thunder Hole.
- Our next stop is the Jordan Pond House for lunch. The parking lot is jammed, so we drop off our wives to get us on the waiting list for a table while Bert and I search for a place to leave the car.
- We walk back from the overflow lot to the restaurant. Carol tells me the wait will be thirty minutes, so I decide to find a comfort station.
- I return and cannot find Carol, Marsha or Bert.
- I finally stumble across Carol, who tells me she was waiting "right over there." I look in the direction she points to see a crowd of what appears to be hundreds of people restlessly milling about until their tables are ready.

- Carol asks me to return to the car to get her phone. I walk back and search the entire car without finding it. I return to the spot where I left her and cannot find Carol, Marsha or Bert.
- Ten minutes later, Carol suddenly appears to say she has been "right over there" the entire time. I look in the direction she points and the crowd now numbers in the thousands.
- Our table finally opens up and we enjoy a pleasant lunch featuring those famous popovers. Afterward, we depart for the trail around Jordan Pond after stopping for a quick tinkle.
- We cut our hike short since we are finding it increasingly chilly in the late afternoon shadows and decide to return to the car, taking the long route through the restaurant so we can make a pit stop before heading back to our B&B.

WEDNESDAY

- Before leaving MDI for home, we drive to Bass Harbor in order to take a glorious afternoon cruise around the outer islands of Blue Hill Bay. After passing the lighthouse, we see harbor and gray seals, eagles, egrets, heron, gulls, and cormorants; idle near the pens of a large salmon farm in the bay, and explore the contents of a lobster trap our guide pulls onboard. We envy all of these creatures since they can urinate with abandon whenever they want, whereas we're trapped on this boat for the next two hours.
- Once we return, three of us dash toward the free-standing sanitation stations at the end of the dock. Carol insists on wanting to use a "proper bathroom." I pull up the directions to our dinner destination -- a lobster pound as we exit the island -- which is 26 miles away. Carol says she can't wait that long. I offer to stop twice along the route but she declines, with gas station accommodations also below her standards, and instead she continues davening in the back seat until we reach the restaurant. The place is mobbed with end-of-season diners, and before Carol tells me her order she dashes off to attend to her urgent need. I am left in the midst of a frenzied hoard of shellfish-crazed gourmands who batter me from side to side as they push their way to the front of the line where they select their dinner and then back into another line to choose their

sides and pay. When Carol returns she finds me in a daze from the pummeling I've taken. All I can mutter is, "... french fries or coleslaw..."

THURSDAY

- That morning, although I put up more of a fight, Bert thrashes me on the tennis courts yet again. We return to clean up before it's time to take him and Marsha back to Portland for their trip home.
- As part of our ongoing quest to discover the ultimate lobster roll, we target a shack located along our route to the airport. Despite the hours posted on their website, we find a "CLOSED" sign on the door. Just as we dejectedly turn away, one of the owners pops his head out from a neighboring building and tells us to step inside; he's still got everything up and running and will be glad to serve us.
- We place our orders and mosey out onto a small patio to await our food. Within minutes, trays are in front of us and we each take big bites to compare notes. Let me tell you, these lobster rolls are unquestionably the...

Oh, dammit -- I have to go to the can. Back in a few.

<u>My Search for Happiness (on Google)</u>

"For every minute you are angry you lose sixty seconds of happiness."
-- Ralph Waldo Emerson

- **But for every day you are angry, you can probably get out
  of making dinner.**

"Happiness is when what you think, what you say, and what you do are
in harmony." -- Mahatma Gandhi

- **Misery is when people insist on harmonizing about how
  happy they are.**

"Happiness is a warm puppy." -- Charles M. Schulz

- **Right up until the moment when something else warm
  comes out of that puppy.**

"When one door of happiness closes, another opens, but often we look
so long at the closed door that we do not see the one that has been
opened for us." -- Helen Keller

- **I presume she was speaking figuratively here.**

"A table, a chair, a bowl of fruit and a violin; what else does a man need
to be happy?" -- Albert Einstein

- **And so Einstein put rumors of his affair with Marilyn
  Monroe to rest.**

"Life is really simple, but we insist on making it complicated." --
Confucius

- **So true -- in addition to the original cereal, you can now
  buy Life in Cinnamon, Vanilla, and Pumpkin Spice.**

"I'd far rather be happy than right any day." -- Douglas Adams

- **But it's tough to keep your chin up when the boss insists you're wrong every single day.**

"Everyone wants to live on top of the mountain, but all the happiness and growth occurs while you're climbing it." -- Andy Rooney

- **For those who remember Andy Rooney, he looked like he never climbed a set of stairs -- much less a mountain.**

"That man is richest whose pleasures are cheapest." -- Henry David Thoreau

- **Try telling that to my wife when I suggest we go to Arby's on date night.**

"A well-developed sense of humor is the pole that adds balance to your steps as you walk the tightrope of life." -- William Arthur Ward

- **And also helps you tolerate extended metaphors.**

"Happiness consists of living each day as if it were the first day of your honeymoon and the last day of your vacation." -- Leo Tolstoy

- **Makes you wonder why his best-known novel wasn't published under the title, "Sex and Booze."**

"In the midst of movement and chaos, keep stillness inside of you." -- Deepak Chopra

- **Which is why I'm refusing to get up from the couch to unload the dishwasher.**

"The right way is not always the popular and easy way. Standing for right when it is unpopular is a true test of moral character." -- Margaret Chase Smith

- **Oh, how the body politic has changed.**

"You may find the worst enemy or best friend in yourself." -- English proverb

- **Me is not on speaking terms with Myself, but I and Me get on like gangbusters.**

"If you hear a voice within you say, 'You cannot paint,' then by all means paint and that voice will be silenced." -- Vincent van Gogh

- **Not if you don't spread a drop cloth and spackle the walls first.**

"Our greatest happiness does not depend on the condition of life in which chances placed us, but is always the result of a good conscience, good health, occupation, and freedom in all just pursuits." -- Thomas Jefferson

- **Compare Jefferson's erudition to this tweet:**

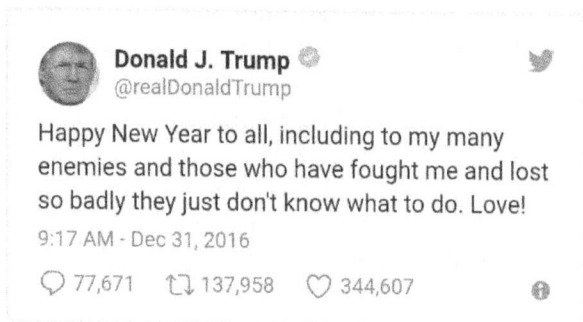

Donald J. Trump
@realDonaldTrump

Happy New Year to all, including to my many enemies and those who have fought me and lost so badly they just don't know what to do. Love!

9:17 AM - Dec 31, 2016

♡ 77,671   ↻ 137,958   ♡ 344,607

Image courtesy of a certain federally-archived Twitter account.

At Least Three of these New Year's Resolutions are Sincere

1. Let my friends and family members know how important they are to me, by stack ranking them.

2. Stop yelling, "OW!" and then giggling every time I nibble on a piece of sharp cheese.

3. Admit that when I say, "I'm going ice fishing," it just means I'm sucking the last of the bourbon off the cubes at the bottom of the glass.

4. Get around to losing those 30 extra pounds before my next birthday.

5. Hmm... seeing that my next birthday is less than 2 weeks away, maybe the one after that.

6. As part of that attempt -- eat healthier. Step 1: start sprinkling turmeric on my ice cream.

7. Accept the things I cannot change, have the courage to change the things I can, and gain the wisdom to recognize the difference between parsley and cilantro.

8. Be more open to the opinions of others, and hear them out before trashing them for their ignorance.

9. Start every day with a dream and then just keep hitting the snooze button.

10. Give up on my goal of teaching the cats to use the toilet, since I don't always make it there myself.

11. Stop and admire the natural beauty that surrounds us before Donald Trump manages to obscure it all in a thick cloud of coal dust.

12. Appreciate all that I have been given and ask only for what you have that I don't.

13. Treat my wife with all the love and affection she deserves, especially before she realizes she could have done much, much better.

Defensive Driving Saves Lives but Wrecks Marriages
======

We were recently on the road for six hours in each direction between Maine and New York to see family. I was behind the wheel the entire time so Carol could check Facebook on her phone for friends posting new videos of kittens adorably provoking larger animals without being eaten alive.

While unpacking the car after we made it home, Carol turned to me and said, "You are a defensive driver." I offered my thanks for her compliment. "You misunderstand," she responded -- "I don't mean that you drive well; I mean that you can't accept any criticism regarding how you handle the car."

I was rather flummoxed by her observation and asked her to provide some examples. "You pass people on the right." I said that was only when some fool in the far left lane was going too damn slow. "You drive too fast." I reminded her she was just as anxious to get home as I was. "You fiddle with the radio and take your eyes off the road." I told her I could not tolerate any country music, had recently become a big fan of hippity-hop, and would listen only to tunes of that genre.

"This is what I mean! You have an excuse for every bit of your obnoxious behavior!" I responded she was welcome to take over the driving duties any time if she felt she could do better. She sighed while saying, "You continue to prove my point," and then walked into the house, leaving me to bring in our overnight bags, her hanging clothes, a half-eaten bag of potato chips, several empty pouches of M&Ms, and the seven pairs of shoes she'd packed for our two-night visit.

But after letting her ~~bitching~~ comments sink in for a bit, I decided to practice what she'd preached and make an effort to become a less frantic, more considerate driver. I had to run a number of errands yesterday and spent a fair amount of time on various roads. Every time someone was merging onto the Maine Turnpike, I moved into the left lane to provide them with a clear path rather than gunning it to get ahead of them. When a car was trying to turn onto the street from a parking lot, I slowed and signaled them to pull out in front of me instead of rolling past and further delaying their egress. When the light changed on a two-way street, I flashed my lights to permit the opposing driver to complete a left turn before I proceeded through the intersection. I have to admit -- I felt more relaxed behind the wheel and didn't even bother to change the station when Fetty Wap's raspy rap faded and Kenny Chesney's tremulous voice came through the speakers.

Last on my list was to pick up Carol at work since her car was in the shop. Because of all the courtesies I'd extended and the measured pace I'd traveled throughout the day, I ended up arriving a half-hour later than she expected. But I figured once I told her how I'd taken her words to heart and embraced a more responsible approach to being on the road, she'd understand and be pleased that I'd turned over a new leaf.

I was wrong about that. "What took you so long?" she asked as I hopped out and went to open the passenger door for her. I said driving at the posted speed limit, while safer, also took a bit more time. "Why didn't you let me know you were running late?" I pointed out that keeping my focus on the road meant I couldn't allow myself to be distracted by texting or talking on the phone. "I'm going to miss the start of my yoga class, so you'd better hurry up and get me there as quickly as possible." I stated that as long as I was driving I had no intention of putting her in harm's way by rushing to get anywhere. Carol looked at me and said, "Fair enough," before pushing me out of the way, jumping into the driver's seat and taking off toward her appointment.

The setting sun illuminated the evening sky with brilliant pinks and purples, and I drank in the peaceful vista while trying to flag down a ride from passing motorists who obviously could have benefited from the same insights recently shared with me about what constitutes courteous driving. As the temperature dropped and I started to shiver from the cold, I hoped that Carol was following her own advice and wouldn't allow herself to become distracted by calling to see where I was; also she'd driven off with my phone still in the car. Once I realized no one was going to stop for me, I had an epiphany while jumping out of the way of the cars that hugged the shoulder: the safest way to drive was to not drive at all. I would gladly turn over all responsibility for being behind the wheel for future trips to my life partner.

And just wait until she hears what I have to say about the way SHE drives, from the comfort of the passenger seat.

Section 4: Blowing A Gasket

<u>Roll With It</u>

You see these kinds of stories in the advice columns all the time; I read one recently where a wife's entire world was turned upside down when her husband of ten years came out to her as a trans woman. Partners who have built a life together, a cooperative existence consisting of mutual interests, shared desires and responsibilities, common bonds strengthened by an inviolate level of trust -- all of a sudden there is a reveal by one member that blindsides the other and leads to an implosion within the relationship.

We experienced such a moment yesterday. Out of the blue, out of nowhere, without any prior hint of concern or something being amiss -- Carol told me she wanted to use a different kind of toilet paper. At that moment... I had no words. I now understand how bedrock feels after being fracked.

We are creatures of habit. Oh, sure -- sometimes we're lured by a sale, or make use of a competitor's coupon – but, minus these rare exceptions, we have been buying the same brand of toilet paper for the entire time we've been together. You've seen the ad where they compare the lengths of various rolls? In our case, the roll reaches back well into the last century.

When Carol was pregnant we talked about potential baby names. One of the names I floated for consideration was "Scott". Carol gave me a puzzled look: "Where did you come up with that? We don't have any 'Scotts' on either side of the family tree." I held up both palms while saying, "Let me finish. If it's a boy, his first name will be 'Scott' -- and his middle name will be 'Tissue.' Just think about it -- all we have to do is let the company know how dedicated we are to their product and his college education will be paid for!" To this day I still flinch at the memory of the withering look Carol shot my way.

I think the genesis of this usurpation may be a comment a family member made when he was here for a visit a few months ago. He came out from the bathroom and declared, "I see you're still buying the kind of toilet paper where I have to use the entire roll to clean myself." I felt his dilemma was more attributable to a long-standing Metamucil addition than how we chose to stock our bathroom, but Carol may have processed his observation differently.

This brings us to the new world I am facing today. We stock up on our brand, purchasing it in bulk at the warehouse store and taking up half the linen closet for storage. It will take some time to deplete our current inventory so I'm going to suggest we implement a phased transition plan, alternating between units of old and new so certain sensitive parts of the anatomy are not chafed by an abrupt change and can ease into the new regimen.

And I've skipped right over the biggest issue here: how are we going to screen potential replacements? What are our acceptance criteria and test plan? Will we use some sort of weighted measure, an assemblage of factors including price, comfort, absorption and -- I'm not sure if this is industry jargon -- "product residual"? This brings back distressing memories of a performance review I suffered through at work years ago, where a capricious manager arbitrarily altered the balance among my evaluation metrics at year's end, resulting in a less than satisfactory effectiveness rating and precluding any salary increase. Sitting through that review was a lengthy and unexpectedly painful episode from which there was no escape. Similar to our relative's complaint regarding his time in our bathroom.

That work experience really rubbed me the wrong way. I hope to avoid a similar sensation when selecting our new brand of TP.

Have you ever been exposed to other people? Or do you know someone who has? If so, you may be entitled to compensation.

If you have experienced any of the following, you are a victim:

- Sadness
- Confusion
- Disappointment
- Loose stools
- Any reality programming featuring a Kardashian
- Skin rash
- Unexpected flatulence
- Heartbreak
- Visits with in-laws

If you, a friend, family member or complete stranger have ever been around people, contact our firm to learn about your rights to life, liberty, and the pursuit of entitlement. There are no fees or expenses for our services unless we claim you won.

DANGERS OF LIVING

Life is fraught with risks that you were not informed of. The manufacturer of human beings failed to adequately warn people about the dangers associated with becoming a member of society and exposure to the foibles of others. Studies indicate that every single day you remain alive you are statistically more likely to die in the future.

To reduce the risks associated with living amongst others, doctors recommend you take steps including healthy eating, regular exercise and accepting responsibility for the consequences of your actions. However, the long-term embrace of these routines increases the possibility of extending your lifespan and thereby your odds of accidentally consuming kale chips, twisting your ankle, or investing in a multi-level marketing "opportunity."

History has shown that an overwhelming majority of cases result in settling rather than holding out for a verdict of true happiness. But some cases result in a trial, where testimony from parents, siblings, life partners, employers, and neighbors presents a picture of an individual so myopic and self-centered that we may choose to terminate representation without prior notice and just leave you to flounder on your own.

QUESTIONS ABOUT LIFE

Why do I have to put up with everyone else? You don't -- that's what we're here for. Our firm will represent you in all situations: grocery shopping, oil changes, responding to unsolicited emails. You can remain firmly ensconced in your cocoon and binge watch *Pretty Little Liars* until your eyes pop out of your head.

How did this happen to me? It's not your fault. Well, not <u>entirely</u> your fault.

Where have all the flowers gone? This one *was* your fault; you planted annuals instead of perennials. You might get a few "volunteers" but after that early spring hail storm don't count on it.

When will I get what I deserve? Soon, my darling -- soon. Just a few more forms to sign.

SETTLEMENT PROCESS

The settlement process starts with putting you in touch with a so-called "therapist" who may or may not be subject to state or federal regulation. You could be offered interventions including but not limited to: mood inhibitors, chiropractic treatment, daily affirmations, requests for a small loan until payday, cupping or gummy vitamins. You may be encouraged to engage with additional therapists, either in sequence or simultaneously and not covered by insurance, depending upon the particulars of your situation. While therapy may result in improvement, there is no guarantee you will experience positive results. Nothing we suggest is intended to diagnose, treat, cure or prevent any future disappointments with your mother.

FACTORS THAT AFFECT SETTLEMENT AMOUNTS

Aspects of a life-related lawsuit that influence a settlement range from personal hardships to rumors that others wish you would "just drop dead already." If evidence clearly shows that living negatively affected your quality of life, in addition to documentation such as report cards with snide behavioral comments from teachers or written warnings from your workplace spelling out consequences "up to and including termination," you will have a better chance of a higher settlement. Residents of AL, DC, ID, KY, OK, SC, WV or Weehawken, New Jersey may have lesser prospects.

Call now -- lines are open but hearts and minds will close quickly.

Double Indumbnity

[SPOILER ALERT: I'm about to reveal essential plot details to a movie released in 1944. If that's going to upset you, then go back to watching *The Sixth Sense*. BTW -- the kid can see Bruce Willis because he's dead.]

Exhausted after a recent day filled with kayaking, yard work, and contemplating the increasing possibility of a Trump presidency, Carol and I collapsed on the couch after dinner and sought some televised (cable-cast?) entertainment. I noticed a listing for a so-called "classic" film; one that I had never managed to see before and so thought we might enjoy it.

The movie was *Double Indemnity*, a leading example of the genre known as *film noir* (which is French for "not in color"). While I enjoy movies and my personal experiences in viewing them go back many decades, I don't consider myself a "film buff" (which is English for "watches movies while naked"). To that end (pun not intended), I've skipped a few chances to see some of the classics, but now I could rectify at least one such oversight and watch a commercial-free showing of a flick that made the top half of the American Film Institute's list of "100 Greatest American Movies." Well, there's no accounting for taste... Here's what happens:

An insurance salesman played by Fred MacMurray is shot after... wait a second -- this movie is about an INSURANCE SALESMAN? I thought the lead characters in these *noir* films were gangsters, or private investigators, or crooked cops. Why would anyone want to watch a drama about an insurance salesman? I'm certain if Arthur Miller had named his play *Death Of An Insurance Salesman* there would have been no Pulitzer awarded and Marilyn Monroe wouldn't be part of his biography, either.

Anyway -- MacMurray staggers into his office after being shot and spends the next two hours slowly bleeding to death. As he becomes increasingly diaphoretic, he musters barely enough strength to talk non-stop through the remainder of the movie, even when he's not in the scene. In a series of flashbacks, we learn what sparked the events leading to the shooting -- which was apparently Barbara Stanwyck's proclivity for receiving unannounced visitors to her home while wearing only a bath towel. After eyeing less skin than I've seen displayed by some Walmart greeters, MacMurray falls hard for the dame. After two more brief meetings, some allegedly clever banter (for example -- *Her*: "I was just fixing some iced tea; would you like a glass?" *Him*: "Yeah, unless you got a bottle of beer that's not working."), and a shot of bourbon, Fred expresses his love for Barbara by saying, "I'm crazy for you, baby." From the current-day perspective, such language is considered neither politically correct nor feminist-embracing. Today, Fred would need to use an affirmative consent approach by asking, "Do I have your permission to engage in adulterous sex and then proceed to knock off your husband?"

The lovebirds hatch a plot, using Fred's inside knowledge of the insurance racket, to murder her other half but make it look like an accident. Specifically, an accident where the soon-to-be-deceased falls off a moving train. Fred is very precise about the circumstances, saying this is the "only way" to pull off the scam and trigger the double indemnity clause. The husband can't be hit by a car, or fall down the steps, or die of boredom from watching this movie. Through death-by-train, the widow will receive twice the normal payout -- a grand total of $100,000. In those days, that was considered a lot of money. Now that's how much Kim Kardashian gets paid for tweeting what brand of eyeliner she wears during liposuction.

Of course, these carefully laid plans start to unravel once Edward G. Robinson gets involved. Ah, finally -- a gangster makes an appearance! Now this is getting interesting... wait, what's that you say? Edward G.'s character is a... CLAIMS ADJUSTER?

- Q: Is there any kind of character that could possibly be less engrossing than an insurance salesman?

- A: Yes. A claims adjuster.

At least Eddie G.'s character is an adjuster with some brains, which he proceeds to use to uncover the scam. Well, actually he doesn't rely on his brains so much as pointing to his chest and saying "the little man inside" provides the insights. If this film were remade today, Robinson would be playing a character with schizoaffective disorder, with the dramatic tension deriving from his ability to connect the dots only when he goes off his meds.

Somewhere in there Stanwyck's step-daughter and her no-good boyfriend come into play. When their involvement threatens to derail the scheme, MacMurray manages to get them out of the picture (pun intended) by greasing the boyfriend's palm with a nickel and encouraging him to make a phone call -- problem solved (I'm not kidding). Carol had briefly fallen asleep (I can't imagine why) during this part of the film, so when the boyfriend later became essential to the action she had no idea who he was and kept peppering me with questions regarding what was happening. I responded by adopting a *noir* persona of my own and told her, "Shut up, baby. I'll fill you in when I'm good and ready to and not a second before. Now go skip into the kitchen and see if you can scare me up a beer that's not working."

Fred MacMurray wasn't the only person who got shot down that evening.

A Test of Our Friendship

I'm interested in making some new friends, so if you would like to be considered for this illustrious honor please complete the following screening questionnaire and promptly return it to me. You should expect to hear results within 4 – 6 weeks; due to the anticipated overwhelming number of responses, only those who merit further consideration should expect a reply. If you make it to Round 2, remember to bring your money order and emergency contact information.

Who are you supporting in the upcoming presidential election?

1. Hillary Clinton
2. Donald Trump
3. Bernie Sanders
4. Jill Stein
5. Gary Johnson
6. Planning to write-in for "The Estimable John Branning" because you want your vote to count for something.

Which of the following toppings do you prefer on your pizza?

1. Pepperoni
2. Banana peppers
3. Extra cheese
4. Whatever you like is fine with me, John – and no, I *insist* you take the last slice.

On a warm summer's day, nothing is more refreshing than:

1. An ice-cold IPA from one of Maine's award-winning craft breweries, served in a chilled pint glass and accompanied by a bowl of that Asian snack mix with the wasabi peas in it.
2. The satisfaction derived from bringing my new friend John another ice-cold IPA and refilling that bowl of Asian snack mix.
3. No. 2 above, but after removing the strangely-shaped white cracker-like things with the black stripes in them because maybe that's seaweed?
4. Nos. 2 & 3 and then not overstaying my welcome.

My idea of showing a friend a good time includes:

1. Doing whatever he wants to do.
2. Not doing things he doesn't want to do.
3. Nos. 1 & 2
4. Nos. 1 & 2 plus bringing over ice-cold IPAs and Asian snack mix without being asked.

Friendship is:

1. A way to explore mutual interests with another person.
2. A one-way street, of which I should be on the giving end and expect little in return.
3. An honor bestowed upon me by someone (initials "JB") who flatters by allowing others to bask in his reflected glory.
4. All of the above plus readiness to pick up the check.

Fill in the blank: "I would take _____ for you."

1. a bullet
2. the rap
3. your suit pants to the dry cleaner
4. it on the chin
5. this survey

BONUS ESSAY: In precisely twelve words, describe why you deserve to have the honor of my friendship bestowed upon you. Please include the words "This," "would," "literally," "be," "the," "greatest," "thing," "that," "could," "happen," "to" and "me" in your response:

_____ _____ _____ _____ _____ _____ _____ _____ __
__ _____ _____ _____!!

By submitting your entry, you are agreeing to the following Terms and Conditions:

- I am licensed to drive and carry my own insurance.
- I have a high-def (or, even better, 4K) television with a minimum screen size of 60", measured diagonally, and subscribe to all the premium cable channels.
- There is always Gifford's ice cream in my freezer.
- I will not bother you with unnecessary texts or tag you in any Facebook posts.
- If it will improve my chances of becoming your friend, you are welcome to use my boat anytime.

Thanks for your entry and good luck!

A Christmas Peril

(With sincere and genuine apologies to Clement Clarke Moore.)

'Twas the night before Christmas, when up in Trump Tower
The Pres-Elect watched TV in the wee hours.
The Donald was hung, he'd proclaimed to the land,
We shouldn't be misled by the size of his hands.
Priebus and Ryan were all snug in their beds,
While visions of disruption danced in their heads.
Kellyanne with her bleached hair, and Bannon with stubble,
Continued to plot how to cause so much trouble.
When out on Fifth Avenue arose such a bleat,
The Donald stopped what he was doing, mid-tweet.
He'd sign on again later to call Baldwin a hater,
But now he descended his gold escalator.
The moon on the breast of the new-fallen snow
Reminded Sir Trump where his hands should not go.
When what to his wandering eyes did appear
But his Cabinet members, who gave him a cheer.
(But not old Chris Christie, face round and waist thick --
The brain trust decided that he was a dick.)
More rapid than denying the impact of hacking
He whistled, and shouted, thanking them for their backing:

"Now, *Zinke*! Now, *Pruitt*! Now, *'Mad Dog'* and *Haley*!
You know I'll embarrass you all almost daily!
And *Tillerson*! You know you're controversial,
But I'll sell them on you like an Exxon commercial.
There *Puzder*! My labor guy! (How I love your name.)
Hot chicks in bikinis are what brought you fame.
And *Pruitt*! I don't give a damn what the tree-huggers say,
Get started dismantling that vile EPA.
There's *Ross*! He's my Commerce guy. He's almost 80.
(I won't let him ponder on issues too weighty.)
Ben Carson for HUD! My black friend -- that's you!
Between you and Kanye, I'm now up to two.

Who's that with head bobbing? Oh, there you are, *Mitt*!
You thought I'd give <u>you</u> a job? Ha, you dumb shit!
There's more of you out there; don't yet know all your names,
But soon at your shuffling feet I'll lay blame."

Trump was chubby and plump, like an orange so ripe,
And I laughed when I saw him, giving him reason to gripe.
With a wink of his eye and a twist of his head
Soon gave me to know I had so much to dread.
He spoke many words, 'cause he knew all the best ones,
And walked back inside, arm in arm with Jeff Sessions.
And brushing his hair back on top of his pate,
He returned to his Twitter account to berate.
But I heard him exclaim, in words no longer puzzlin' --
"Happy Christmas to all, and to hell with the Muslims!"

<u>Are There Nuclear Codes For Launching An F-Bomb?</u>

When our son Josh was in the eighth grade, he came home from school one afternoon with his report card. "How'd you do?" I asked. He hung his head for a moment and then said, "I got six 'A's and one grade I need to talk to you about." While I really would have preferred to focus on the six stellar assessments, I told him to proceed with his tale of woe, which was that he'd gotten an "F" in English. "How could you fail English?!" my wife protested. I advocated for a calmer response, suggesting perhaps his intention was to replace use of his native tongue with proficiency in a new language. Carol looked at me, not saying a word but with a glance that spoke volumes, then turned her attention back to Josh and again demanded, "How could you fail English?!" I was hopeful that Josh would demonstrate his mastery of, perhaps, French, and explain to his *mère* that he understood she had just issued a plaintive *cri de coeur*, but *une seule langue n'est jamais suffisante*.

That did not prove to be the case. Josh received the failing grade because he didn't turn in a project about common grammatical and spelling errors. The sidebar here is that I met with his teacher and convinced her to let him hand in the assignment late, and she in return would adjust his grade for the semester to a minimally-passing "D" as long as he met all the report's requirements. He did, and she did, and that's the closest our son ever came to getting straight As in his entire academic career.

The reason I relate this tale is to lead into a discussion of some of those sticking points of grammar that he (meaning, "Me, standing over him with a whip in one hand and sharpened stick in the other") included in his finished paper. Even though this incident happened years ago, I continue to see people making these same mistakes. While I recently called my senator to strongly express my objection to Betsy DeVos becoming Secretary of Education (hashtag resist), if she can get our children (or even just our President) to understand the difference between "lose" and "loose," I'll continue to protest her appointment but will no longer drop any f-bombs while doing so.

Here are some of those grammatical conundrums from Josh's long-ago assignment, and my current-day attempts at un-drumming them:

➤ What is the difference between **less** and **fewer**?

- Use "fewer" when describing something you can count (example: "Beyoncé's masterful 2016 album *Lemonade* won <u>fewer</u> Grammys than Adele's treacly *25*."); use "less" when describing something you can't count (example: "I think even <u>less</u> of Metallica after seeing them perform with Lady Gaga."). However, there are several exceptions to that rule, with this being among the most notable:
    - *"How do I love thee? Let me count the ways."* If you were able to count the ways but only got up to one (especially if that one was, *"I love it when you leave me alone."*), you should say, *"Hmm... I guess I love thee <u>less</u> than I thought."*

➤ When should I use **their** versus **there**?

- The good news is you can use them interchangeably in the same sentence, as long as you are trying to console someone:
    - <u>Their</u> <u>there</u>, son. We still love thee, even if you failed English. Just a little <u>less</u> than we used to."

➤ Does it matter if I use **your** instead of **you're**?

- Hell yes! "Your" is a possessive pronoun and is used when pairing an owner and object. "You're" means "you are," and is the pairing of a noun and verb. People get these mixed up, writing things like, "After a report card like that, <u>your</u> no child of mine," and, "Go talk to <u>you're</u> *mère* because I want nothing more to do with you right now."
- "You're" is properly referred to as a contraction, and that's where the confusion comes from. When Carol was in labor with Josh, the doctor wanted to know how close together the contractions were. I asked him to clarify his question, since

"you'll" and "you're" are much closer together in the dictionary than, say, "aren't" and "weren't."

- I also berated him for pelting us with grammatical questions when we were their to have a baby. After that, we saw a lot <u>less</u> of him.

Josh did go on to study French in high school, and as a result knows most of the major swear words *en français*, along with slang for certain body parts. I know this because I've heard him express himself thusly over the years. You know what they say about the study of language: Use it or loose it.

Eleven Reasons Why I Hate To Go Grocery Shopping

I had five items on my grocery list this morning and had to go to SEVEN different stores to find everything. Can you sense the seethe coming off what I type below?

1. No matter how many times I write it down, I never remember to pick up those special boxes of baking soda for removing odors in the refrigerator.

2. Why is there more than one kind of toilet paper? There are only two things that we do involving a toilet (which, and not by coincidence, are named "Number One" and "Number Two") - so *maybe* you could talk me into two kinds of toilet paper, but that's it.

3. Why are the various locations of one grocery store chain laid out differently? When I pop into a Hannaford's -- ANY Hannaford's -- I want to know exactly where to find limes, diet tonic water, and gin. My time is precious; it's hot outside and I want to get home as quickly as possible to cool off on the deck with a refreshing G&T at my side. As I walk into the store limes should be prominently displayed in a produce section located immediately to my right -- not to the left, not toward the back, not in a bin located fifty feet away from the other citrus fruits. Get it together, Hannaford's.

4. Did you know the supermarket chain named in #3 above is actually called "Hannaford"? Everyone around here calls it "Hannaford's", so they should change their name already. The other predominant chain around here is "Shaw's", not "Shaw." Learn from your competition, Hannaford's.

5. I've lost count of how many different sizes of shopping carts there are. Let's see: there's the traditional "buggy;" then there's a compact, more square version of said buggy; there's a buggy with built-in rear-facing double child seats so your kids can fling Cheetos at me while you're bent over to grab a tub of private-label mayonnaise from the bottom shelf; there's the hand-held plastic basket and then there's another plastic one with an extendable handle and wheels built into the bottom so you can drag your groceries around, mere millimeters off of the Cheetos-dust-encrusted tile floor, and then there's the mobility-

impaired electric cart with the buggy up front that is entirely too long for users to drive around the end of each aisle without either crashing into a display of canned goods or clipping me right on my Achilles tendon. Some stores now offer a service where you order your groceries online and they'll bring them out to your waiting car; no navigation required. That sounds promising in theory but they still make me come inside the store for the gin, so what's the point?

6. Why are there both "salted" and "unsalted" butter? The next ingredient in any recipe that calls for unsalted butter is... salt.

7. And don't get me started on milk. Skim, 1/2%, 1%, 2%, whole, ultra, organic, lactose-free, soy, rice, almond, non-GHO and those UHT packages that aren't in the dairy section and have a shelf-life only slightly less than that of canned soup.

8. And SOUP! Oh my GOD! I want a can... of... tomato... soup. Not "light," not "Tuscan," not "reduced sodium," not "bisque," not "hearty," not with "basil" or "coconut." I want the soup my mother used to serve me along with a grilled cheese (made with white bread, blackened on one side, using the slices of yellow American processed cheese food that come individually wrapped) that she cut on the bias so I had points to daintily dip into the bowl.

9. Dear checkout person: just because I've come through your line does NOT mean I am interested in having you examine each of my items as you scan them and ask, "Oh, this looks interesting -- what do you make with THAT?" "What's in the bakery bag?" -- None of your damn business. And the next time you ask me if it's parsley or cilantro, I'm going to tell you whichever one is cheaper, OK?

10. Why are the free cookies on the bakery counter limited to just children? They can't even reach the jar without adult assistance.

11. To whoever is parked behind me in the lot: when my backup lights come on, that means I am going to be backing up my car, imminently. Do not then start your car, throw your tranny into reverse and try to beat me into the neutral zone between our rows. Today, so very fortunately for you, I was driving my brand-new SUV and stomped on my brakes to prevent a collision. But the next time this happens it's just as likely I'll be driving my wife's thirteen-year-old junk heap and will not

hesitate to exercise my right of way since I was already established coming out of my spot. I would welcome the chance to slam into your rear end since the impact might actually flatten out some of the dents her car already has. I will leave you to pick up your rear bumper and shattered tail light assembly, as I roll down my window while driving away so you can hear me cackle at your misfortune.

Alright -- I've ranted enough. Time to calm down with that G&T. Oh, bloody hell -- I'm out of diet tonic.

Section 5: Glove Compartment Syndrome

Sinking Relation-ship

My wife Carol said something really sweet and profound to me the other day. I wish I'd muted the TV long enough to catch it all.

Carol starts every day by saying, "I love you." I respond by asking her who she's on the phone with.

The other evening I said I'd light some candles and suggested we take a romantic bath together. Carol said she wasn't up for a bath but would wash her hands with me. Actually, I think she said she wanted to wash her hands of me.

We introduced some role reversal into our lovemaking: Carol said she was too tired, and I said I had a headache.

One point of contention was whether the household duties were being split evenly. I said let's make a list. After I wrote everything down I said I'd done my part, so...

We have a long-standing "joke" the reason we're still together is that neither of us could get a gun permit. But there are knives all over the kitchen -- so it must be love, right?

To keep things fresh, Carol recommended a "date night" once a month. I agreed but find it irritating when the guys honk from the driveway and expect her to run out to the car. Whatever happened to manners?

You'll hear people say things like, "I married my best friend." Well, I bet you and your best friend never had a joint checking account, did you?

I looked at myself in the mirror and saw thinning gray hair, wrinkles, sagging muscles and a paunch. Appearing from behind, Carol wrapped her arms around me and said, "You've really let yourself go."

Some people start the morning by checking the obituary page to see if their name is listed. Carol and I read the letters to Dear Abby and ask each other, "Did you write this?"

Regardless of what we're arguing about, one rule is that we never call each other names. We rely on slang for various body parts.

Carol will tell you she married me because I make her laugh. Several years went by before I realized it's at my expense.

As I write this, Carol and I have been married for 36 years. Many of them happy.

Every so often you'll hear about a couple married for fifty, sixty, seventy-five years and when asked for the secret to their long relationship will say, "We've never argued once." I can say that's true for Carol and me as well -- we've argued many, many times.
How have we managed to stay married for so long? Well, we believe that divorce is not an option. That is, it's not an *affordable* option.

All you need is love. But sometimes a spare bedroom comes in handy also.

This Does Not Compute

The irony in today's subject is that it came to me while listening to streaming music through an app on my wi-fi connected smartphone, which was wirelessly transmitting tunes to the Bluetooth speaker my friend Bert gave me for my last birthday.

Being the cheapskate that I am, I make use of the free version of the music app. This means I must listen to commercials after nearly every song. The ads alternate between exhortations to upgrade to the "premium" version and enticements for other products. Just now I heard a pitch for a wi-fi enabled garage door opener: "If you drive away and leave your garage door open, it sends your phone an alert to close it!" Back when we lived in a house with an attached garage, I received such notifications long before the advent of smartphones and wi-fi -- whenever I headed to work and left the garage door open, my wife would leave a castigating voicemail on my office line letting me know I'd forgotten to close the door "again."

The concept of integrating computing devices into everyday objects and then having them communicate with you and/or each other is known as the "Internet of Things." It's commonly abbreviated as "IoT" or, more colloquially, as "PitA." (If, like me, you are older than the internet, you know what "PitA" stands for.) It is almost impossible these days to purchase any kind of household appliance, or yard machinery, or sign up for pest removal service, and not have a phone app associated with it. Your dishwasher will text you when the pots and pans are clean and dry and ready to be put away. Your lawn mower will update you on how high the grass has gotten since its last clipping. Your exterminator (You have an exterminator? Sorry, but I'll pass on that dinner invitation.) will provide a link to a live webcam so you can see what kind of critters are darting around in the crawlspace under the house. You've likely heard about the latest refrigerators that scan the bar codes on your groceries and generate a shopping list when the milk's gone bad or you're out of Jerusalem artichokes. There are even models with interior cameras, so if your idea of hijinks is to make an unscheduled stop at the supermarket, you can connect with the fridge and confirm what is, or isn't, inside it at that moment. There's nothing like subjecting yourself to the hassle of searching for a too-narrow-to-open-the-car-door space in the supermarket parking lot, steering your buggy through the too-narrow-for-carts-to-pass-each-other width of the aisles, then purchasing a 35-pound bucket of cat litter instead of the gallon of 2% milk you really needed.

You can remotely turn the lights on and off in your house (with special light bulb kits that'll set you back a mere $70); you can get a "smart" thermostat that learns when you like to make a room warmer in winter (when you're in it) or cooler in summer (likewise; it takes cloud computing to figure this out?). And perhaps you've seen the commercials for devices such as the Amazon Echo or Google Home (and of course Apple's is coming soon) which, if you have any semblance of sanity remaining after going through the installation process to ensure compatibility with your router and enabled devices, respond accordingly when you bark out commands like, "I want pizza!" or, "Play some polka music!" or, "Goddam it, where's that pizza I told you to order thirty minutes ago?" You can ask the Echo, "Alexa - tell me a joke," to which "she" responds: "You paid $140 for me, imbecile. The joke's on you."

Here are some other state-of-the-art appliances poised to take their place along with the overpriced, clumsily-functioning, and soon-to-be-found-on-Craigslist devices already mentioned:

- A wi-fi connected tabletop convection oven that recognizes 25 different kinds of food and cooks them automatically. _I_ can't even recognize 25 different kinds of food. Do you still have to take the bacon out of the package to cook it? If so, then what's the point? This oven sells for $1500. Some of you may remember when banks used to give out toasters for free when you opened a checking account.
- A fork that counts how many bites you take, and buzzes in your hand if you eat too quickly. My wife counts how many bites I take, and she buzzes in my ear if I eat too quickly.
- A machine that "simplifies" home beer brewing, so it allegedly takes half the time and half the skill of the usual home brew set-up. While I don't home brew, I know many people who do and have great admiration for their dedication to crafting something

that otherwise can only be found in every liquor, grocery, drug, and convenience store within a stone's throw. This device costs $800. Do you know how many six-packs I could buy for $800? Enough to get through two-thirds of the Labor Day weekend.

- A nonstick pan that provides recipes and tells you when to flip whatever you're making. This device costs $129, and one of the recipes included is for a grilled cheese sandwich (really). I do not need $129 worth of technology to tell me how to make a grilled cheese. There's a fool-proof method to follow here: flip the sandwich over 10 seconds before you smell the pan side starting to burn.

Now, please don't think I'm a Luddite (which, for years, I thought was a fan of the host of the old "Password" game show) -- while I may not be an early adopter, I have enjoyed the benefits of technological advances and internet-based services for quite a while. It's been more than a decade since we dropped our landline in favor of going smartphone-only. I pay nearly all my bills online and step into a bank branch only when I am jonesing for a lollipop and don't have a haircut scheduled. And I mentioned that gift of a Bluetooth speaker, which I use to listen to my favorite artists from the 70s, 80s, but mostly the 70s while cooking, cleaning, or spending time in the bathroom to shower, shave or shi... er, *sit* and read for a while.

But enough is enough. Our dentist recommended we start using a rechargeable electric toothbrush; fair enough, but the brand the practice encouraged us to purchase comes with Bluetooth connectivity, sharing the data with an app to keep track of how often and for how long we brush each day. Honest to God, if someone needs to utilize that level of technology to avoid cavities, then dentures are a foregone conclusion.

Plus, when I check my phone to see how I'm doing, I keep dropping it in the toilet.

<u>Here's Everything I Know About Wine in Five Minutes or (Much) Less</u>

I recently retired, and am making good use of the free time I've gained by ignoring the long list of home improvement projects I promised to undertake and instead deciding to become a wine expert. Or, to use the correct term, an **oenophile**. Let me share what I've learned so far.

The first thing I've learned is the proper pronunciation of that term is "EE-no-file" and not, as I have long thought, "oh-NOFF-phil-lee." But I don't want to cloak myself in a mantle of pretentiousness right off the bat, so I'll refer to myself and others who share my ~~elitist~~ in-depth interest as "winers."

Step One in my journey was to work on developing my pallet. In order to accomplish this, I drove over to the local lumber yard where a very helpful lumberphile clarified I likely meant *palate*. I thanked him for his assistance, got back in the car and headed for the nearest department store, where I was certain I would find a palate in the Housewares department, next to the silverware.

There is a great deal of ceremony that accompanies the ~~pretention~~ presentation of a fine wine, starting with uncorking the bottle. Does the bottle have a cork, and is that cork natural or synthetic? The use of natural corks can lead to a condition called "cork taint," which means if the cork is so afflicted then you tain't gonna serve that wine to nobody. However, these days more and more higher-end vintages are utilizing screw caps. Someone should design a cap making it easier for those with arthritis to open a bottle, like what you find on prescription vials from the pharmacy. Push down -- slight turn -- glug glug glug.

Some believe wine is improved by aerating it, which is the practice of introducing air into the wine. There are devices designed for this purpose, the use of which are recommended versus introducing wine into the air by hurtling a full glass across the room in a drunken rage.

A wine's dryness is associated with the amount of tannin in it. My evaluation of this characteristic is coming along very slowly since all I've been able to discern, in every bottle of wine I've opened so far, is its level of wetness. In an effort to improve my abilities here, I got back in the car and went to a local tannin salon. One hour and $60 later, I wasn't any better at making the distinction but did leave with a new-found appreciation for the importance of sunblock.

Wine has a language all its own. Actually, that's not true -- winers use common English words in unique and innovative ways to describe the characteristics of the fermented grape. In this context, adjectives like "angular," "opulent," and "fallen over" (which is what my wife Carol says happens after I finish my second glass) take on alternative meanings. One surprising designation is "stemmy," since I've always thought Stemmy was the designated frontman for Motörhead. A wine can be described as "chewy;" I, for one, would certainly return any bottle of wine where I had to chew what poured out of it. After delighting in a recent tasting, I told Carol I'd enjoyed a Barbera with great legs that I'd found firm, musky and voluptuous. She immediately filed for divorce, naming "Barbera" as the co-respondent.

I could go on but I've already spent enough time away from my studies. Tonight's lesson plan is to spend the evening exploring a companion I hope to find elegant, supple and a bit racy. And if it turns out Carol has to work late, I'll just move on to a third glass and enjoy ~~tripping~~ ~~tipping~~ tippling on my own.

I'm a Groan-Up

I heated up some alphabet soup for lunch today but quickly lost my appetite -- it had a vowel smell.

Did you know there's a medical term for someone who calls in sick to work and instead goes shopping? It's called mall-lingering.

I told my wife I was polyamorous, and she said fine -- Polly could have me.

Yesterday, upon the stair / I met a man who wasn't there / He wasn't there again today / I wish, I wish my building had an elevator.

A triangle with the sum of its angles exceeding 180 degrees is described as "obese."

I bought a cantaloupe and was very disappointed after tasting it. This made me feel meloncholy.

A group of alligators is called a "congregation." I guess that's because they're Chewish.

Is an actor who auditions for the role of "Courtroom Transcriptionist" hoping to be typecast?

I accidentally fell into a vat of brine and found myself in quite a pickle.

I seem to be interested in lovemaking only when I feel sleep coming on. I guess that makes me a trance-sexual.

Recently I wasn't feeling well but couldn't decide whether I should go to my doctor's office or the emergency room for treatment. So I called 911 and asked them to dispatch an ambivalence.

Ever since falling into an open sewer, I've been antiseptic.

I tried to hike through a swamp in the woods and managed to get stuck in the mud, making a real morass of myself.

I got knocked out during my first boxing match, but that's because I was a neofight.

My eighth-grade English teacher asked me to define "obstreperous" and I shouted, "NO WAY!"

If a psychiatrist ran for political office, could he be accused of voter Freud?

<u>Putting the Angst in Thanksgiving</u>

If you're still trying to decide what to serve for Thanksgiving this year, here are a few favorites from my recipe file. They are guaranteed to please -- and you should remember, in this context, the word "guarantee" has no basis in fact or implies any legally enforceable standard for satisfaction. What are you going to do if you don't like them, or end up in the emergency room as a consequence of ingesting – sue me? I'll see you and your ambulance-chasing huckster attorney in court, sucker. Enjoy!

Turkey ceviche. Have your butcher remove the skin and bone from a 4 to 5-pound turkey breast. Using the same knife you almost sliced your finger off with last Thanksgiving, dice the raw turkey into quarter-inch cubes. "Cook" the diced turkey by placing in a glass or other non-reactive bowl and marinating in 1 cup of freshly-squeezed lime juice; refrigerate for 3 hours. Remove and add finely chopped tomatoes, red onion, celery, green bell pepper, parsley and cilantro and gently combine all ingredients while drizzling with ½-cup EVOO. Season to taste with salt and pepper and a dash of Maalox®.

Chocolate cake stuffing. Using your favorite boxed cake mix, prepare two 9" layers. Sauté chopped onion and celery in butter, then mix in one layer of the cake, crumbled. Add 1 tablespoon each of poultry seasoning and rainbow jimmies. Stuff the bird with the mixture and bake until you realize hours too late that the built-in thermometer has malfunctioned, leaving the turkey completely dried out and beyond salvaging. Save the day by bringing out the second cake layer to serve to your disappointed guests. OPTIONAL: Drizzle gravy over top of cake before slicing.

Sauced cranberries. Open a can of prepared cranberry sauce while sipping chilled vodka, straight up, since that's the extent of your culinary abilities. Have a bandage ready when you inevitably cut your finger on the sharp edge while removing the lid. Sloppily dump contents of can into an antique crystal serving dish, possibly chipping it. Toss onto the table, which will likely break the antique at its base, and then immediately return to the sanctuary of the living room to sullenly keep at it with the vodka until everyone leaves.

Green bean casserole. Par-boil two pounds of trimmed beans, drain and immediately immerse in ice water to preserve their color. Arrange evenly in a shallow pan and pour the prepared contents of one box of lime Jell-O® over the beans. Place dish in the refrigerator until the gelatin sets. Once the mixture has solidified, remove from refrigerator and top with french fried onions. Bring to room temperature on the kitchen counter and then forget to serve with the rest of the meal.

Sweet potato casserole. Boil 11 pounds of peeled and diced sweet potatoes for one hour, or until all traces of color are removed. Drain and mash using a mallet or garden weasel. Stir in the contents of one bag of granulated sugar. (NOTE: For those who require this dish to be sugar-free, you are shit out of luck.) Pour the resulting mush into a Bundt pan that has been lined with mini-marshmallows. (Another NOTE: If you are obtaining the mini-marshmallows by sifting through packets of powdered hot chocolate mix, be sure to rinse all traces of the cocoa from the mini-marshmallows so as not to disrupt the delicate balance of flavors this dish requires.) Bake at 400 degrees for two hours and then invert the Bundt pan. When the casserole refuses to release from the pan, swear uncontrollably for ten to fifteen minutes and then get on with the rest of your life.

Roasted cauliflower and Brussels sprouts with bacon. Thinly slice one head of cauliflower florets and 1-1/2 pounds of Brussels sprouts, lightly season with salt and pepper and then sauté in safflower oil until tender. Separately, pan fry two packages of bacon until crispy and nicely browned. Throw away the sautéed vegetables and serve the delicious bacon to your appreciative family.

Mac and chinos. Prepare a box of macaroni and cheese according to the package directions and serve while insisting everyone wear matching outfits during dinner.

Glazed carrots. Trim two pounds baby carrots, removing tops and tips before peeling, which will result in approximately three ounces of remaining vegetable. Using a small brush, apply several layers of shellac to each carrot stick. Place in a colorful serving bowl and advise these are not to be eaten.

Spiral sliced ham. Combine one cup light brown sugar, 1/4 cup prepared mustard and two tablespoons cider vinegar. Mix thoroughly in a bowl and then drizzle over a 12-pound boneless, skinless cured ham. (What it has been cured of is not important.) Bake in a 350-degree oven for two hours. TO SPIRAL SLICE BEFORE SERVING: Insert the tines of a large serving fork into the center of the ham and secure the handle in the chuck of a 1/2" drill. As you operate the drill, have another family member (preferably your wife's least-favorite uncle) firmly press a sharpened carving knife against the surface of the spinning ham. Involve any children present in the meal preparation by having them chase after the flying pieces of meat and place onto a china platter.

Pumpkin pie. Really? You make your pies from scratch? What a complete waste of time. Just buy whatever brand is on sale, prepare according to the package directions, chip away the burnt edge of the crust and obscure the processed flavor by spritzing half a can of whipped cream on it.

Remember that everything tastes better when it's made with love, which is why so many family dinners are fondly recalled as being inedible.

How Financially Literate are Mainers?

The free-credit-score website WalletHub recently released its report on 2017's Most & Least Financially Literate States. We'll dive into how Maine (where I live) did in a few moments, but here's my first concern with the survey -- the rankings go from 1 - 51, and last I checked there are only 50 states. So, I'm a little dubious of the accuracy of these results...

Oh, now that I'm actually *reading* the report, I see the District of Columbia is included. I dunno -- DC isn't a "state," right? Don't their license plates display the motto "Taxation Without Representation?" Aren't DC and Puerto Rico duking it out over which one of them should become the 51st state?

Anyway -- you can read in the report's "Methodology" section how WalletHub conducted its assessment. Let's go to the video tape... er, I mean -- let's examine Maine's performance:

Maine ranked 4th overall (behind New Hampshire, Minnesota and North Dakota). Not too shabby, eh? There are a number of breakouts included the report; here is Maine's performance in a few of them along with my explanations:

5th – WalletHub's 'WalletLiteracy Survey' Score

- You can take the survey here: https://wallethub.com/wallet-literacy-score. I just took it and my grade was A-minus. I missed 4 out of 30 questions: I was wrong about how to rank sources of lending for higher education from best to worst, misunderstood when I would start being charged interest on a new purchase if I carried over a balance on my credit card, and incorrectly answered questions about my age and gender.

7th – % of Adults Aged 18+ Who Spend More than They Earn

- I'm not sure if this means Mainers are the seventh-highest in the nation at spending <u>more</u> than they earn? Seems like it's better to be ranked higher as someone who spends <u>less</u> than they earn, no?

3rd – % of Unbanked Households

- These are people who are very poor pool players.

5th – % of Adults Aged 18+ Who Borrow from Nonbank Lenders

- "Nonbank" lenders are financial institutions that make only loans; they don't offer savings or checking accounts. Examples of nonbank lenders are Quicken Loans, Freedom Mortgage, and your father's wallet while he's in the shower.

15th – % of Adults Aged 18+ Who Scored at Least 80% on FINRA's Financial Literacy Test

- Another fun test! You will find this finance-based quiz at http://www.usfinancialcapability.org/quiz.php. It's much shorter and (I thought) easier than the WalletLiteracy Survey; I got 6 out of 6 (#6 was a bonus question; I knew the name of both actors who played Darren on *Bewitched*), but again I have a concern with the methodology, since on my results page the nice folks at FINRA (motto: "It's pronounced 'FIN-ruh'!") presumed I was taking the quiz in Alabama.
- It does seem odd that Mainers did better on the more comprehensive WalletLiteracy Survey than on FINRA's simpler test. Maybe this was just because we didn't completely fill in the little ovals using a #2 pencil.

23rd – % of Adults Aged 25+ with at Least a Bachelor's Degree

- I am 25+ (plus plus plus...) and do not have a Bachelor's Degree. This is largely because I have not been a bachelor since 1981.
- While I hold higher education in great esteem and have respect for those with advanced degrees -- some of the people I know

with the absolute <u>worst</u> ability to manage their personal finances have MBA's and Ph.D.'s. Go figure.

Now that we are armed with these insights, let's see how we improve in the rankings on next year's report. My money's on Maine walking all over North Dakota to take over the #3 slot; anyone reading this want to get a piece of that action? It's a sure bet.

<u>Save Time by Ignoring These Household Hints</u>

Look for the tabs on either side of a box of aluminum foil and press them in -- they keep the roll anchored, so when you go to rip off a sheet you don't pull the entire roll out of the box.

- If you forget to press in those tabs and the entire roll comes out of the box, drops off the counter and unfurls the length of the kitchen into the dining room, you can choose to either waste the better part of a day trying to roll it back up, or just bring your misery to a quick end by slicing your wrists on the serrated edge of the box.

When making your own guacamole, place an avocado pit in the container to keep it colorful longer.

- It's possible to stab yourself in the hand, nearly severing a finger, when trying to remove the pit from an avocado with a very sharp paring knife.

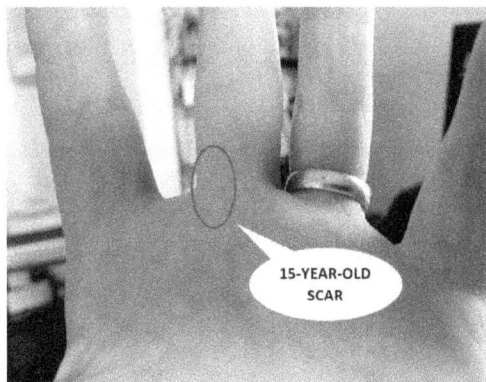

15-YEAR-OLD
SCAR

Store cottage cheese upside down in the original container. This forces air out and keeps it fresher.

- Make sure the top is securely reattached before turning the container upside down.

You can use a pair of pantyhose as an emergency replacement for a broken fan belt in your vehicle.

- It was a complete coincidence I happened to be wearing a pair of my wife's pantyhose the day I utilized this tip.

When a light bulb breaks in the socket, slice a potato in half and use it to grip the broken section. Twist gently to unscrew the damaged bulb.

- Do not use that same half a potato to then make home fries.

If you've spilled red wine on your clothing, remove the stain by sprinkling with salt and then covering with club soda. Let it sit overnight before laundering.

- Mix the remaining club soda with scotch and ice and sip throughout the evening since your wife suggested you lay off the wine for awhile.

Boil orange peel and cloves to get rid of unpleasant smells in the kitchen.

- Fry some onions to get rid of the overwhelming smell of orange peel and cloves.

Place a few drops of essential oil on the cardboard tube of a toilet paper roll to make your bathroom smell wonderful.

- As long as you don't let anyone actually use your bathroom.

There are at least <u>five</u> different ways to pit cherries!

- Which is why I stick with applesauce, right out of the jar.

Clean your barbecue grill with a wad of aluminum foil.
- Which is all you can do with it once you forget to push in those tabs and the roll escapes its cardboard confines, refusing all attempts at reintroduction into polite society.

Be sure to ~~avoid~~ look for the next article in this series, with answers to common cooking conundrums such as:

- When a recipe calls for canola oil, can I substitute 10W30?
- What the hell is "Cream of Tartar"? And why does it come in such a big container when all I ever need for anything is 1/8th of a teaspoon?
- What other uses are there for sour milk, other than pouring it on my husband's cereal the morning after he's spilled red wine all over the place?

Section 6: Battery Terminal Illness

Settling the Snore

Carol woke me from a sound sleep last night, shaking my shoulder and saying in an urgent whisper, "There's someone in the house."

I leapt out of bed and headed for the closet. "Where are you going?" Carol shouted. "To hide," I responded. "The baseball bat is under your side of the mattress."

"Do you still have your earplugs in?" she asked. She then informed me she had not said, "There's someone in the house" but instead "Your snoring is so loud." "Jee-zus..." I muttered under my breath. Well, it sounded like a mutter to me because I still had my earplugs in but she claimed I hollered, which she did not take kindly to.

I returned to bed, where I now inferred a delineation between "her side" and "my side". I presumed Carol was upset about the shouting and that I hadn't been more aggressive in my defense of her and our home, but please keep in mind:

1. I was sound asleep and wasn't permitted any time to process her comment, preferably while being offered coffee and a sweet roll.
2. There was no actual threat underway.
3. I believe men and women to be equals; therefore she could have taken the initiative to chase off the interloper. And did I mention the bat was on her side of the bed?

Adrenaline was now coursing through my system as a result of the incident; that, combined with the fact Carol had quickly gone back to sleep -- and, in a cruel irony, immediately started snoring -- unsettled me to the point where I got up again and headed downstairs to watch TV until I felt calm enough to return to bed.

On my way through the kitchen in the dark, I stepped in a puddle of something lukewarm and sticky, which I knew from experience was the gift of cat regurgitation. I cleaned up the mess from the floor and my bare foot and headed for the couch. I wanted to avoid bright lights at that wee hour and so was navigating around with only the glow of my cell phone to guide me. Now I needed to find the remote for the television. This is often a challenge when Carol has stayed up later than me since she has a tendency to leave it "wherever" on her way to bed. Sometimes it's on the coffee table, sometimes the ottoman, occasionally the bathroom sink, and once I found it in the refrigerator next to the water pitcher. This time I was fortunate to spy it on one of the end tables and turned on the set.

Once the cable box and television had come to life, I heard sound but saw no picture. I flipped up and down a few channels and all were sound-only. I hit the "guide" button to bring up the program display and saw a string of detail-free "Not Available"'s in place of the listings. "Cable's on the fritz again," I thought to myself. "Great..." I then recalled I could perhaps watch via the cable company's app on my tablet. I stumbled back up to the bedroom to retrieve it from my bedside table. Carol was still asleep/snoring and I don't believe heard me cry out another "JEE-ZUS!" when I banged my shin on the corner of the bed frame. Tablet in hand, I banged my other shin when leaving, adding His middle initial and last name to my excited utterance, and gingerly hobbled back downstairs.

I booted up and was pleased to find the app permitted me to view the entire channel array, with picture and sound intact. Since the tablet's speakers are small and tinny, I broke out my noise-cancelling headphones and plugged them in to listen with richer timbre to the snappy dialogue of a *Law & Order* rerun. I flicked on the headphones and heard nothing -- dead battery, urrgh. I went back into the kitchen to grab a replacement, stepping in another cat puddle on the way. After completing that clean-up I returned to the couch, swapped out the battery, placed on the headphones and returned to *L&O*. Except by now the episode had ended and some reality show was already in progress. In this program, a couple who may or may not be legally married, each with children from multiple prior relationships, runs an upscale boutique employing an alarming number of heavily-tattooed and oddly-coiffed men and women, some of whom appear to be "transitioning" (to and from what was not clear to me). Rather than actually working, this crew appears to stand around the shop ridiculing their co-workers and bitching about any customers who are foolish enough to wander in during the day. Not surprisingly, the business is losing money ass-over-teakettle, so some titan of industry who apparently has enough spare time on his hands to step away from his Fortune 500 company to appear on this show serves as a "consultant" to the business in an effort to stem the flow of cash going down the drain as he collects a hefty fee for his alleged services. All this while everyone quaffs from a seemingly endless supply of champagne.

I scrolled through the other channels but could only find infomercials for products I had no interest in buying or other "reality-based" programs I had no interest in watching. At this point, I decided to give up the ghost and turn everything off, thoughtfully leaving the remote behind one of the couch cushions so Carol could find it. I tip-toed upstairs once again, stepping on a suspiciously warm spot of carpeting but lacking the initiative to investigate further, and stealthily slid under the covers while putting my earplugs back in. Carol was still snoring, so I added an additional layer of soundproofing by placing a pillow sham over my head. Just as I started to doze off, our cat Miles decided to take up residence on the sham, curling his eleven pounds into a ball pressing down on the side of my face. I tossed both sham and cat toward some undefined location on the other side of the bedroom and attempted to settle back in for some much-needed sleep.

With my return to a restful state now mere breaths away, Carol's alarm went off. She rolled over, hit the snooze and, by the sound of things, immediately went back to sleep. I sighed deeply and attempted to relax again, at which point the alarm rang for the second time. After three more snooze cycles I gave up, getting out of bed for good and heading downstairs to prepare the morning pot of coffee. I skidded on a puddle of you-know-what while grabbing filters from the cabinet.

While waiting for the coffee to brew, I went to watch the morning news. Where was the remote? In my fuzzy state, it took a few minutes before I recalled its placement behind the cushion. I turned on the set and went back to the kitchen to pour myself a cup of java -- of which there was none because I'd forgotten to turn on the machine. After correcting that oversight, I realized Carol was still sleeping and went upstairs to make sure she got up in time for work. I shook her shoulder and said, "There's a burglar downstairs." She didn't stir, so I leapt up on the mattress and began bouncing around, landing on the floor on her side of the bed with a thud. Startled awake, she asked what the hell was happening. I said I'd just come up to check on her and let her know the coffee was almost ready. She eyed me suspiciously, saying she'd be right down. I returned to the kitchen, smirking all the way back since I'd now exacted my revenge for a poor night's sleep.

I was pleased with myself right up until the moment I found hot coffee flowing all over the counter since in my exhausted haze I'd also neglected to place the pot under the drip basket. You know what they say: "You snooze, you lose." In my case, I'd lost a night's sleep, a full pot of coffee and what little remained of my wife's and one cat's affection for me.

How to Deceive in Business Without Really Crying

I'm pleased to announce the imminent publication of the next volume in my corporate leadership skill-building series: *Business? Fo' Shizzness!* Previous titles that have found their way to the top of the remainder pile include:

- *Workplace? More Like Jerk-place*
- *How To Get Your Dream Job Without Actually Falling Asleep During the Interview*
- *Your Employees May Be Abusing FMLA -- Here's How You Can, Too*

I've received some very flattering responses to the earlier books; witness these testimonials:

- "I found your last book very helpful when I was unexpectedly 'separated' from my last employer. At 487 pages in hardback, it left quite an impression when I smacked my supervisor over the head with it while being dragged from the building."
- "After reading your article, 'Ten Sure-Fire Ways to Lose a Job,' I took it to heart and vowed to make changes in my behavior at work. It worked! Now I am unemployed and LOVING IT!!"
- "I always discover something of value in your publications, John. The last time I thumbed through one at a yard sale I found a $2 bill that someone had been using as a bookmark."

I've been in the business world for quite some time now and have conducted my fair share of interviews (it's like hosting a talk show, but instead of chatting with movie stars you find yourself sitting across from their accountants) and managed plenty of people (much like herding cats, but with less success). Here's a preview of the new book's Chapter MCXVII -- Whether You Live To Work Or Work To Live, I Still Need That Report First Thing Tomorrow Morning:

1. See how your candidates react to the unexpected. Experts recommend arriving ten minutes before the scheduled start of an interview. Once your prospects are announced, storm out of your office and demand to know why they are twenty minutes late. If you can keep a straight face throughout their flustered apologies, so much the better.

2. Ask if they would like something to drink before getting started. If they say no, reply with, "Too bad -- I hate to drink alone," and break out a bottle of Scotch. If they say yes, slide a can of Moxie their way.

3. Do not hire anyone who brings lunch to an interview. Unless it's a salad; all the business etiquette guides say to stick with something that comes in small bites you can eat with utensils.

4. Ask this, then sit back and get ready to watch a mind being blown. "What would you do if someone asked you a hypothetical question during an interview?"

5. Here's an easy way to identify those false "accomplishments" listed on a résumé. Rip it up and ask the candidate to hand-write a new one on the spot.

6. Learn to use open and closed questions appropriately. An example of the former is, "How early are you willing to come in to open the office?" An example of the latter is, "How late you can stay in order to close the office?" Follow up with probes to uncover more information, such as: "In that case, can you bring me coffee in the mornings?" and "Do you really have anything to go home to after work?"

7. Positive reinforcement drives stronger performance. An example is telling your team you are positive they will all lose their jobs if sales don't increase by 30% in the next quarter.

8. "A leader is a dealer in hope" -- Napoleon Bonaparte." "A dealer is a leader in dope" -- Napoleon Dynamite.

9. If you want to get more out of your people, you've got to put more into your people. That's why offices have so much junk food laying around.

10. The best interviews are two-way conversations. The worst interviews are when the hiring manager enters the conference room eighteen minutes late with a half-eaten donut in hand and says she's running behind so "this will have to be short."

BONUS! You've surely seen this so-called "inspirational" chart more times than you can count:

TEN THINGS THAT REQUIRE ZERO TALENT

1. Being on time
2. Work ethic
3. Effort
4. Body language
5. Energy
6. Attitude
7. Passion
8. Being coachable
9. Doing extra
10. Being prepared

Here are some additions to that list, offered here exclusively and guaranteed to be equally as useless:

TEN <u>MORE</u> THINGS THAT REQUIRE ZERO TALENT

1. Using a napkin
2. Opening a door
3. Licking a stamp
4. Making toast
5. Pointing at things
6. Walking while chewing gum
7. Being a Kardashian
8. Riding in a car
9. Eating potato chips
10. Compiling lists like this

If this preview hasn't encouraged you to open your wallet for my new book, then you are far smarter than I am normally willing to give credit for. You wouldn't be looking for a new job by any chance, would you?

Model Patient

I've had some periodic trouble with my wrist and so recently returned to the orthopedist. He had me run through the symptoms; upon deciding it was similar to prior episodes he recommended the same course of treatment, telling me "you should be the poster boy for cortisone injection."

Hmm... I'd never seriously considered a modeling career before but from what I've read this is how the beautiful people are discovered, randomly through such happenstance. So-And-So was behind the counter at the Dairy Queen; Such-And-Such was standing in line at the Motor Vehicle Bureau. In my case, a licensed physician -- someone who is board-certified in his ability to recognize the optimal condition of the human anatomy -- indicated I was a paragon of photogenic excellence. Therefore I've decided to strike while my best years are still ahead of me.

While I don't read the glossy magazines, only glancing at their covers while waiting to scan my instant oatmeal and frozen pizza through the checkout line, I am aware of a recent appreciation for male celebrities who display what's referred to as a "dad bod." I easily meet, if not exceed, that standard: flabby but not yet gone completely to seed; a soft roundness from which emanates a certain *je ne sais quoi* imparted through a casual approach to shaving and personal hygiene. Fashion is all about identifying trends in advance of widespread acceptance, as documented through their eventual appearance in a Target ad, so I think there's some life yet to be rung out of this physical archetype.

I've also gleaned that in order to launch my new career I'll need agency representation. I'm familiar with Ford, Elite, and Wilhelmina but I think I need something more boutique-y. There's a fellow who runs a Glamour Shots booth at the local mall who I've often seen critically assessing female passers-by, staring at them intently before asking whether they've given any thought to becoming a model. I overheard him offer one such candidate a "private session." I need to pick up a prescription at CVS anyway, so I think I'll kill two birds with one stone and saunter past his set-up to see if he's accepting new clientele.

I'm sure it's easy for you to scoff at my dream and consider this a "vanity project" -- but let me assure you that's the farthest thing from the truth. Celebrity, when managed effectively, can be a springboard toward becoming a force for positive societal change. Josh Duhamel, Ian Somerhalder and Kellan Lutz are just three of many famous former male models I had never heard of before Googling "famous former male models." I'm reasonably certain, now that I see Wikipedia says these fellows appear in movies and on television, they are donating some of their newly-acquired fortunes to charity, if only for the tax break. Once I begin to appear on posters as a notable endorser of cortisone injections -- striking a variety of pain-followed-by-relief poses in order bring to the attention of our youth-obsessed culture this effective treatment for conditions including arthritis, frozen shoulder and gout; on display in the examination rooms of every orthopedist and neurologist along with that clinic in Florida where the teen who impersonated a doctor worked -- fame will quickly follow, and after indulging in just a few modest self-congratulatory purchases I'll associate myself with a worthy cause, hoping to become as well-known for my good works as my good looks. I want to be thought of as more than just another pudgy face.

I do hope the cortisone starts to kick in soon, since before staging my audition catwalk past the food court I'd like to grab some lunch at Panda Express, and with my wrist being what it is I still can't properly grip the chopsticks.

Twenty-two Signs I Am Not Aging As Gracefully As I'd Like

1. More and more frequently, when I come out from the grocery store I can't remember where I parked the car.

2. When I use the trimmer to clean out my ear and nose hair, the battery dies before I can finish.

3. The default volume for the television is set to "27."

4. I still watch television.

5. It sometimes takes me two tries to get up from the couch.

6. After cutting the grass, I have to take a nap.

7. After my second beer, I have to take a nap.

8. I've started to drive in the passing lane on the highway in order to keep those behind me at what I consider a reasonable speed.

9. I'm hungry for dinner at 4:30.

10. I submit a letter to the editor of my local newspaper about some issue or other at least once a week.

11. I still get a newspaper.

12. I know who the Doobie Brothers are, and have seen them in concert within the last year.

13. Now that Jane Pauley has taken over as host of *CBS Sunday Morning*, I'm concerned the show is starting to skew too "young."

14. I can't distinguish among the various Kardashian sisters.

15. I recall when a tablet was something you took, versus something you read a book on.

16. I recently became friends with someone -- IRL.

17. Grocery store brands are "good enough."

18. I remember seeing Susan Sarandon in her film debut.

19. I take ibuprofen before anything even starts hurting.

20. If you offer me a Budweiser -- instead of turning up my nose and insisting on a craft brew, I will drink it.

21. I remember when there was no 3-point shot in the NBA.

22. If I can't get up from the couch after two tries, I just stay put and turn the TV back on.

My Bathroom Innovation Will Make You Flush with Excitement

"Honey," I say, taking my wife's hands in mine and looking into her eyes with all the affection I can muster, "I love you with all my heart. Keeping that in mind, I want to let you know the next time I go to use the bathroom and find a roll of toilet paper with only three sheets left on it -- I'm leaving you."

She tells me she doesn't want to waste the remaining paper by throwing it out unused. I respond by asking what exactly can three sheets of toilet paper be used for? I suggest if thrift is her concern then perhaps she could use it to blow her nose, or remove some lipstick, or wipe the smudges off her phone screen, and then install a fresh roll with a clear conscience. She says those all sound like silly suggestions to her. I offer another suggestion: if she doesn't come up with some solution -- soon -- then the next time this happens I will signal my displeasure by using those three sheets to start a small bonfire in the loo.

She says that's ridiculous. I counter that it's no more ridiculous than leaving a useless remnant of a toilet paper roll in place and expecting the next occupant to assume the responsibility for replacing it at a particularly inconvenient moment.

She says I'm not being fair; there are plenty of times when she finishes the roll and replaces it with a new one. I concede that *sometimes* she does that, but that leads to another concern -- why do I find the empty cardboard centers perched on the edge of the sink? "It's recyclable," she informs me. "Yes," I acknowledge. "I am well aware of that and applaud you for your sensitivity to the environmental impact. But this is my question: how exactly do you expect that roll to be introduced into the Reuse-Reduce-Recycle triad without actually placing it in the recycling bin?"

She responds that she *intends* to place the empty roll in the recycling bin but occasionally just forgets. I remind her that the road to You Know Where (we used to say "Hell," but now we say "the Trump White House") is paved with good intentions. She looks at me with exasperation and asks why I am making such a big deal out of such a little thing. I say the future of our planet is not a "little thing." She tells me she's getting tired of dealing with my hyperbole. I tell her I'm getting tired of her unwillingness to consider how finding three useless sheets hanging limply, or a forlorn cardboard tube teetering on the edge of the sink, and then having to deal with those situations ON TOP OF everything else I am responsible for around the house drives me nuts.

Now the gloves come off. She asks me just WHAT exactly are all my "responsibilities" around the house? I start to tick off the list: empty the dishwasher, scoop out the cat litter, do all the laundry that's OK to go in the dryer, refill the bird feeders that she can't reach... I tell her I'm just providing the highlights here; there are more but at the moment I am taken aback by her challenge to recite it all from memory. Then I offer this clincher: "There are LOTS of things I take care of that YOU WON'T HANDLE." A slight smirk slowly spreads across Carol's face as she composes her response: "What exactly do you have to deal with that I can't take care of myself?" I look her straight in the eye and state, "I handle paying all the bills, and I file our taxes every year. I've never seen you even TRY to sign into our online banking or the tax program, much less take care of the monthly bills or our annual returns." Carol smacks herself in the forehead while rolling her eyes and says, "That's because you're the one who set up all the computer-based accounts WITHOUT TELLING ME WHAT ANY OF THE PASSWORDS ARE! I've asked you to write them down for me and you NEVER DO!" I inform her that writing down passwords is not a secure way to share them. I think I see a look of disbelief on her face just before she turns away from me. I realize that, correct as I may be, I have trod onto thin ice and attempt to gingerly work my way back to safer ground.

"Honey," I say, with all the affection I can muster, "I'm not trying to start an argument here."

"Oh, I think it's too late for that."

"Well... be that as it may. Let's see if we can come to an agreement -- you accept your responsibility for replacing the toilet paper and getting the empty roll all the way into the recycling bin, and I'll promise to try and not shrink your yoga pants again. Doesn't that sound reasonable?"

Carol's been up in the bedroom with the door locked for several hours now, so she must be giving my proposal some serious thought. I've been using this time productively by unspooling all the rolls of toilet paper stored in the linen closet and writing "REMEMBER TO PUT ME IN THE RECYCLE BIN! :-)" with a marker on the cardboard cores. I'm also reverse-numbering the corners of the sheets so it's clear when we get down to those last three useless squares. I just hope I can get all the paper wrapped back around the tubes before she comes downstairs. I can't wait to witness her response to my latest innovation in the name of household efficiency.

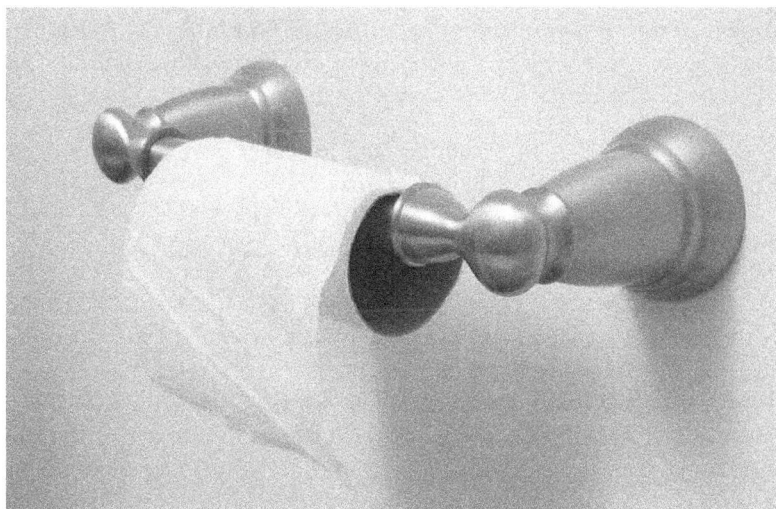

Photo courtesy of the aggrieved author.

Grammar and Grampa

There are elements of speech and grammar and certain turns of phrase I just can't keep straight, no matter how many times I watch the series of "Comma Queen" videos online. Here are some of the challenges that currently flummox me:

Flounder vs. **Founder**: I think of one of these as a fish and the other as someone who… found something. Yet "flounder" also means to flail about (like the fish, I guess) and "founder" is used when something sinks like a stone (let me illustrate with this example: "The career of the *founder* of American Apparel *foundered* after both employee morale and the company's finances *foundered*." Makes sense now, yes?) This brief rhyme may help to clarify the distinction:

> A flounder may founder
> A founder may, too.
> The difference between is
> Confusing to you.

Verb tenses: I become increasingly tense when trying to identify the various forms of verbs. All I recall from the days I didn't cut English class is that there are three different verb tenses – past ("I *went* to the store."), present ("I *go* to the store.") and future ("JEE-zus! I *just went* to the store and now you want me to *go back again*?"). However, there are additional verb tenses to which I must not have been introduced while cooling my heels in detention, including:

- Present Perfect (This is the condition Grandma insists she is in when the family tries to convince her to move to an assisted living facility.)
- Past Perfect (Confusingly, also known as "Pluperfect." Am I the only one this strikes as a made-up word? Maybe someone meant to say "Plumpernickle," as in the bread. Which is also known as "dark rye", so go and try to make sense of that.)
- Future Perfect (This is what Donald Trump is promising.)

Depending on which resource you care to explore further (Or should that be *farther*? Because you want to get as much distance between yourself and these confusing explanations as possible.), there are claims of there being only TWO and as many as THIRTEEN different verb forms. Here's an actual definition from one grammar site, attempting to explain a particular verb tense that, according to the Heisenberg Uncertainty Principle, ceases to exist the moment I start to discuss it:

- "The past perfect progressive (continuous) is used to describe an action that started in the past and and was still in progress when a second action started. Both actions began and ended in the past."

(Before I offer an example, let me point out that the description above actually displays "... and and was still in progress..." -- on the website of a company trying to sell you software to check your grammar.)

Anyway, here's an example of a sentence describing an action that started in the past that was still in progress when a second action started:

- "By the time any of this verb talk started to make sense to me, I **had been dying** for at least twenty minutes."

Remember, the proper use of this specific verb tense means the second action also ended in the past, which in my example means at this moment either: 1) I'm already dead, or 2) regardless of how Maine's Governor Paul LePage feels about it, somebody administered Narcan to me.

Fewer vs. **Less**: "Fewer" is used to describe things you can count, while "less" is used for things you can't. As an example: "I couldn't care *fewer* about that" is absolutely correct since, if given sufficient time, I can come up with <u>exactly</u> how many ways I couldn't care about whatever "that" is referring to. Plurhaps how many different kinds of bread there are.

Use of the apostrophe: Apostrophe was the Greek goddess of love. We use her name to form the words "apostle," "posture," "trophy," and "fee for services rendered." It's also the source of a common phrase derived from French – "*Apropostrophe* of nothing, he started to ramble on about pronouns as if him knew everything about the subject and me knew nothing."

If you have any additional insights to share via comments that may unflummox me farther, please feel to do so. Or don't so. Or do-si-do, if you prefer to dance around the subject.

Weakend Plans

Whereupon a carefully calibrated three-day weekend devolves into chaos and disappointment faster than the Cruz-Kasich alliance:

Weekend Frustration #1: My wife loses a pair of costly Ray-Ban sunglasses while we are out kayaking on the lake during a balmy Friday. They are perched atop her cap while she uses one of two identical pairs of binoculars we recently purchased to check out the thrilling sight of eagles circling above our position. As she tracks them climbing higher and higher, and her head tilts back farther and farther, the sunglasses reach the tipping point, tumbling back and slipping into the depths of the lake. She is disconsolate; I say I hope she can find some solace in using one of the four other pairs she has scattered across her purse, the house, and our car.

WF #2: My observation is not warmly received.

WF #3: On Saturday morning we get up shortly after sunrise in order to make an hour's drive to a state park to join in an early morning bird walk. However, in order to arrive on time we needed to get up <u>before</u> sunrise – so we arrive just as the cadre of punctual attendees begin to disappear into the woods. Hustling to catch up, I trip over a prominent tree root. Fortunately, I am not injured. Unfortunately, this is because my fall is broken by landing on my new pair of binoculars. Several of the birders come to check and make sure I'm OK; I assure them I am fine and the only things damaged are my pride and binoculars. One fellow asks what brand they are; when I tell him he replies, "Oh, those are <u>useless</u> for birding – no loss there." I spend the rest of the walk bereft of any magnification assist, squinting across the width of fields and up toward the tops of trees trying my best to zero in on a vast array of migratory birds, the sighting of which brings delight to all but me since I can't spot any of them. My bird journal for the day remains a blank page.

WF #4: Early Sunday morning we wake up later than planned and therefore have to hustle to get to a fundraising race in which we are participating, arriving just in time to get registered and take our places at the start. There is an announcement to let people go out in order of speed and ability so we let the runners go first, then the joggers, then the families pushing strollers, then someone with a two-legged dog in a cart, and finally we cheer on a few elders using walkers before we join in to pass through the starting gate. Along the route we see a mother and toddler ambling together at a pace set by the little one's short strides -- except when their progress is interrupted by a series of tantrums (the toddler's) where she plants herself at the side of the road and moves again only after several minutes of her mother's cajoling. They still finish before we do.

WF #5: After completing the race, crossing the finish line at such a slow pace that the chips embedded in our numbered bibs are fooled into thinking time is reversing, we drive another 100 miles to a factory outlet store that is closed when we get there. I recheck its Facebook page, which clearly displays Sunday hours. I rattle the locked doors in the hope that, despite the darkness inside, there are employees sitting idle and just awaiting some sort of provocation to leap into action and let us in to commence shopping. This does not prove to be the case, so we stand around flummoxed for a few minutes before accepting we are S-O-L and will need to return another day to make our purchases. Trying to salvage something from the day's long haul, and since we are already so many miles from home, we decide to drive even farther to a restaurant where we'd enjoyed a fantastic lunch during a road trip one Saturday a few weeks before.

WF #6: We arrive at the restaurant and discover they are closed for lunch on Sundays. We give up on any further adventures and head for home, feeling grateful for the relatively low price of petrol these days since we've burned through most of a tank over the weekend with little to show for it. Stopping at our neighborhood gas station to fill the tank, I pull out my phone to make use of the app for payment that offers a ten-cent-per-gallon discount...

WF #7: ... and watch helplessly as the phone slips from my fingers and falls to the ground, shattering the screen. Now every time I take a glance at the weather forecast I'm alarmed by what appears to be an impending electrical storm, with streaks of lightning covering the screen.

The Final Weekend Frustration: It comes to an end too quickly; another Monday rolls around...

Section 7: A Failure of Catalytic Proportions

There are words I've been using my entire life and then, in one horrifying moment -- usually during a presentation to senior management, or when I accepted my Nobel Peace Prize -- will discover I've completely misunderstood their meaning.

Exacerbate is one of them. I always thought it meant to improve a situation (as in, "Those three scotch and sodas I had before dinner really exacerbated my mood."), only recently learning it means the exact opposite, to make a situation worse (as in, "Those three scotch and sodas I had before dinner really exacerbated my mood.").

Mitigate is another. I thought offering up a defense of "mitigating" circumstances meant I should get off scot-free, whereas it actually means I'm still just as guilty of whatever I was accused of but might pay a fine instead of serving time in the slammer. I also learned as recently as typing that last sentence that it's not "scott-free."

Then, of course, there are the Toxic Twins of **flammable** and **inflammable**, which sound like opposites but mean the same thing. In first grade, we learned to "Stop, Drop and Roll" if we ever caught on fire, and how our pajamas should be treated to ensure they wouldn't burst into flames if our teenaged siblings fell asleep while sneaking a smoke in the bedroom. I ran home after school and asked my mother if the Batman PJs she'd just bought me were *inflammable*. "Of course they are, dear," my mother replied -- "I insisted on it." We had a difficult relationship.

I used to use **nonplussed** to express how something didn't faze me, that I took in stride. When I found out it means precisely the opposite I can describe my reaction only as... nonplussed.

And I've never understood how, if **capitulate** means to surrender, why **recapitulate** wouldn't mean to surrender again. Let me know if I need to repeat that last observation.

And it's not just the meaning of various words; sometimes there is a relationship between objects that surprises me. I recently learned **capers** are actually **pickled flower buds**. And **cilantro** and **coriander** come from the same plant. Or that **Donald Trump** has a sister who is a **respected federal judge**.

There -- I'm *nonplussed* again. Where's the scotch?

How I Know I Had the Worst Cold Ever...

There was nothing "common" about the cold I just got over. Here's how I know:

- My head snapped forward and back so violently when sneezing, the National Highway Traffic Safety Administration had me give demos for their crash test dummies.
- I was so stuffed up, a taxidermist commented on how life-like I looked.
- I went through so many trees' worth of tissues, Julia Butterfly Hill unfriended me on Facebook.
- I drank so much chicken soup, all across the country matzo balls were left stranded high and dry.
- My eyes watered so much, I placed a rain barrel next to my side of the bed.
- I sneezed so hard, I launched a loogie that struck one of the cats in the head and knocked it unconscious.
- My voice got so low and raspy, Tom Waits asked me to be his vocal coach.
- I blew my nose so frequently, I jump-started a wind turbine.
- I sucked on so many cough drops, the Smith Brothers came back from the dead to revel in their second fortune.
- I gargled with so much salt water, ocean levels dropped a foot.
- My nose ran so much, I bought it a pair of sneakers.
- I drank so much tea, I sprained my wrist from dipping the bags in the teacup.
- I popped so many decongestants, I'm now on the DEA "Watch List."
- I took so many supplements with Vitamin C, orange juice futures closed at an all-time high.
- I smeared on so much Vicks VapoRub, I'm planning a swim across the English Channel.
- My ears were so plugged up, I thought Mariah Carey sounded fine on New Year's Eve.
- I hugged the hot water bottle so tightly, my wife is naming it a co-respondent in her divorce filing.

But the ultimate factor that tipped the scales to "worst ever" is because it was MY BIRTHDAY in the midst of the period I wrestled with this affliction. Didn't want to drink or party one little bit. Well, now that I'm finally on the other side of the experience I plan to make up for it this weekend.

Stay tuned for my next post: "How I Know I Had the Worst Hangover Ever…"

No Rhyme or Reason (well, it rhymes a little bit)

Comey was fired; it came as a shock.
Right in the midst of an FBI probe.
Now the department will be run ad hoc
Until Donald J, wandering in his bathrobe,
Decides who its next fearless leader should be.

But once he gave ol' Jimmy Comey the can
The President said that we all soon would thank him.
And while the courts pick apart his Muslim ban
He lets the whole world know that no one outranks him.
Just like Sally Yates -- didn't need her, you see.

The President's staff said 'twas all about Clinton,
How Comey said there were no grounds to indict.
Which contradicts at what the Donald was hintin'
When he, in his letter, brought Russia to light.
Three times, so he claims, he was told he was clean.

The Democrats cry out together, as one,
This firing echoes an evil Nixonian.
The GOP doesn't see storm clouds, but sun
Although there's a handful that call it draconian.
More hearings in Congress will surely convene.

What are we to make of this Tuesday Night Massacre?
How will this impact the Federal Bureau?
Is that Kellyanne on the tube? We can ask her.
While others require explanations more thorough.
There's no lesson learned when there's no one to teach.

Just months ago, Trump shook his hand and then praised him.
"He's become more famous than me!" he was quoted.
But don't let him think you are one who betrays him;
If seeking the truth, then you're quickly demoted.
How soon do you think there's a vote to impeach?

<u>Goal All The Way</u>

"Success is the ability to go from one failure to another with no loss of enthusiasm." -- Winston Churchill

- **No wonder Churchill was in politics, since that kind of attitude got me dismissed from several prior positions in the "real world."**

"The obstacle is the path." -- Zen saying

- **Turn around and head back to the car. -- Just saying.**

"Whenever you see a successful person, you only see the public glories, never the private sacrifices to reach them." -- Vaibhav Shah

- **And aren't we all thankful for that?**

"Success? I don't know what that word means. I'm happy. But success, that goes back to what in somebody's eyes success means. For me, success is inner peace. That's a good day for me." -- Denzel Washington

- **I like Denzel as much as the next guy, but he should stick to a script.**

"Opportunities don't happen. You create them." -- Chris Grosser

- **Hence some unverifiable entries on my résumé.**

"Great minds discuss ideas; average minds discuss events; small minds discuss people." -- Eleanor Roosevelt

- **I'm more of an *Us Weekly* fan, but I get your point.**

"A successful man is one who can lay a firm foundation with the bricks others have thrown at him." -- David Brinkley

- **I don't believe our local building codes permit this.**

"There are no shortcuts to anyplace worth going." -- Beverly Sills

- **Sounds like someone who should download Waze.**

"No one can make you feel inferior without your consent." -- Eleanor Roosevelt

- **These affirmative consent guidelines on college campuses are really getting out of hand.**

"If you're going through hell, keep going." -- Winston Churchill

- **Hang a left when you reach resignation and then take the exit for despair.**

"Don't be afraid to give up the good to go for the great." -- John D. Rockefeller

- **Rockefeller made his fortune scooping up all those abandoned goods at rock-bottom prices.**

"Happiness is a butterfly, which when pursued, is always beyond your grasp, but which, if you will sit down quietly, may alight upon you." -- Nathaniel Hawthorne

- **Break's over -- back to work.**

"If you can't explain it simply, you don't understand it well enough." -- Albert Einstein

- **Oh, I understand it perfectly -- it's my <u>boss</u> who's no Einstein.**

"There are two types of people who will tell you that you cannot make a difference in this world: those who are afraid to try and those who are afraid you will succeed." -- Ray Goforth

- **There are actually three types of people but I'm afraid to tell you about the third one.**

"Start where you are. Use what you have. Do what you can." -- Arthur Ashe

- **Canadian doubles is for sissies.**

"It is necessary for us to learn from others' mistakes. You will not live long enough to make them all yourself." -- Hyman George Rickover

- But, in my case, not for lack of effort.

"Any activity becomes creative when the doer cares about doing it right, or better." --John Updike

- **Any activity becomes better when it includes Dewar's and soda.**

"Eighty percent of success is just showing up." -- Woody Allen

- **So why then is 50% of my bonus tied to productivity?**

"Be wiser than other people, if you can; but do not tell them so." -- Philip Dormer Stanhope

- **What if I say I received "anonymous complaints" that they're all dumb as rocks?**

"The speed of a runaway horse counts for nothing." -- Jean Cocteau

- **Unless you're the horse.**

"The future belongs to those who believe in the beauty of their dreams."
-- Eleanor Roosevelt

- **The present belongs to those who believe in marrying the beauty of their dreams.**

"One of the advantages of being disorderly is that one is constantly making exciting discoveries." -- A.A. Milne

- **"Look – I found clean underwear in the bottom of the laundry pile!"**

"The bravest are surely those who have the clearest vision of what is before them, glory and danger alike, and yet notwithstanding go out to meet it." -- Thucydides

- **I'm happy to be certified as second-tier brave and just go out to meet the glory.**

"Fortune favors the brave." – Terence

- **I'll settle for a 60/40 split since you handled all the danger stuff.**

"One of the lessons of history is that nothing is often a good thing to do and always a clever thing to say." -- Will Durant

- **"   !"**

"No one ever gets far unless he accomplishes the impossible at least once a day." -- L. Ron Hubbard

- **This is why Hugh Hefner is so grateful for Viagra.**

"Genius is one percent inspiration and ninety-nine percent perspiration." -- Thomas Alva Edison

- **Remember he said this before indoor plumbing was in wide use.**

"The cure for boredom is curiosity. There is no cure for curiosity." -- Ellen Parr

- **A fatal diagnosis if you're a cat.**

"All good things which exist are the fruits of originality." -- John Stuart Mill

- **That's great, since I <u>hate</u> vegetables.**

"The person who makes a success of living is the one who sees his goal steadily and aims for it unswervingly." -- Cecil B. DeMille

- **Unlike the elderly gentleman driving the Cadillac in front of me.**

"It does not matter how slowly you go so long as you do not stop." -- Confucius

- **Confucius – I'm going with Cecil. You can ride with Gramps in his Coupe deVille.**

"The best way to make your dreams come true is to wake up." -- Paul Valery

- **Believe me -- waking up because it's time to go to work is not a dream come true.**

"You'll always miss 100 percent of the shots you don't take." -- Wayne Gretzky

- **Hasn't this been adopted as the motto of the NRA?**

"The dreadful burden of having nothing to do." -- Nicolas Boileau

- **Here's something to keep you busy -- try writing in complete sentences.**

"I learned much from my teachers, more from my books, and most from my mistakes." -- Anonymous

- **Mistake #1 - forgetting to sign your name to this insight.**

"A wise man will make more opportunities than he finds." -- Sir Francis Bacon

- **Breakfast irony: one can never make enough bacon.**

"Measure twice, cut once." -- Craftsman's aphorism

- **Count your fingers immediately afterward.**

"What is harder than rock, or softer than water? Yet soft water hollows out hard rock. Persevere." -- Ovid

- **And yet when you throw a hard rock into soft water, it sinks right to the bottom. Perplexing.**

"If I have seen further than others, it is by standing upon the shoulders of giants." -- Sir Isaac Newton

- **Admittedly, at the risk of pissing off the giants.**

"When in doubt, win the trick." -- Edmond Hoyle

- **Is this about Bridge or prostitution?**

"I not only use all the brains that I have, but all that I can borrow." -- Woodrow Wilson

- **You weren't using yours, anyway.**

"There is no disinfectant like success." -- Daniel J. Boorstin

- **A co-worker keeps rubbing my nose in his success -- but come to think of it I haven't caught a cold in, like, three years.**

"Nothing succeeds like success." -- Alexander Dumas

- **Or, apparently, disinfects.**

"The secret of successful managing is to keep the five guys who hate you away from the four guys who haven't made up their minds." -- Charles "Casey" Stengel

- **Remember this before you sign up for another "Leadership Skills" workshop.**

"Being a hero is about the shortest-lived profession on earth." -- Will Rogers

- **Nope – "Special Assistant to the CEO" is.**

"The manner in which a man chooses to gamble indicates his character or his lack of it." -- William Saroyan

- **Gamble? Never. I stick to "skills-based gaming."**

"One day Alice came to a fork in the road and saw a Cheshire cat in a tree. 'Which road do I take?' she asked. 'Where do you want to go?' was his response. 'I don't know,' Alice answered. 'Then,' said the cat, 'it doesn't matter.'" -- Lewis Carroll

- **The only directions less useful than these come from Apple Maps.**

"A good solution applied with vigor now is better than a perfect solution applied 10 minutes later." -- George S. Patton

- **If this were true then I wouldn't have had to update my résumé so many times.**

"Clear your mind of can't." -- Solon

- **"Screw you, Solon." -- Kant**

<u>Small Minds Talk About People Living in Tiny Houses</u>

There are several programs on cable dedicated to the "tiny house" movement. Indicative of the creative forces involved with these shows, all feature the word "tiny" in their titles:

- *Tiny House, Tiny Nation*
- *Tiny House Builders*
- *Tiny House, Big Living*
- *Tiny Hands, Tiny House*
- *It's Not 'Tiny,' Doctor – It's 'Ticonderoga, New York'*

Whenever my wife ~~forces~~ encourages me to watch one of these programs, we always marvel at the ingenuity involved with the design and construction of these shrunken abodes. A bed folds into the wall and has stained glass displayed on its underside; a hibachi is retro-fitted for propane and stands in for the stove; the vegetable crisper in the refrigerator doubles as a sock drawer.

(Of course, Maine has been at the forefront of the tiny house movement well in advance of this trend. For generations, we have embraced compactly dimensioned, creatively furnished and three's-a-crowd structures -- we call them "camps.")

And fad aside, "tiny" isn't even the smallest acknowledged house size. According to one industry website, "right-sized" homes are broken down into these categories, from smallest to largest: Micro (~150 sq. ft.); Compact; Miniature; Tiny; Little; Small; Efficiency; Reduced; Downsized (~1000 sq. ft.). These distinctions undoubtedly lead to conversations like this:

- *'Oh, what a darling 'tiny' house you have! Of course, we gave up ours years ago in order to reduce our carbon footprint down to pinky-toe level when we moved into our 'micro' home. It has everything you could possibly need -- the only accommodations we've had to make are to take all our meals at Burger King – have you tried their pancakes? -- and sometimes Nash sleeps in the lounge at the office when he needs a good night's rest.'*

[A BRIEF ASIDE: The term "right-sized" is popular in Corporate America as a euphemism for "Our piss-poor mismanagement of the bottom line means we are laying off dozens, if not hundreds or thousands, of lesser-paid employees so the members of the senior management team can continue to reap their obscene bonuses." As someone often victimized by such action, it made me shudder as I typed it in the paragraph above, even in this context.]

After the big reveal, where the homeowners see their completed domicile for the first time -- usually with a "surprise" flourish like a skylight, or a red wagon from childhood fashioned into a coffee table, or when they now learn for space reasons the kitchen sink and bathtub have been placed outdoors -- they ooh and ahh, and Carol joins in from her vantage point on our couch (a couch which, while modest within the context of our home's layout, could not possibly fit into any of these tiny houses and would be replaced by a reclaimed park bench -- or, as an example of multi-purpose ingenuity in action, by a pair of toilets set side-by-side facing the media center). She'll turn to me (which would be tough from a perch on a toilet, so scotch that idea) and express her desire to design, build and move into a tiny house of our very own. While I hate to harsh her buzz, it becomes my responsibility to point out the following:

1. We already live in a "tiny" house, since our dining room table also serves as a file cabinet, bookshelf, cat bed and ironing board.

2. If she's looking for a small space within which to carry out the functions of daily living, I remind her we already live in one, known as our bedroom. We sleep, eat and watch TV within those four walls and can even enjoy the outdoors from an adjoining deck. Out of discretion I don't also include, "and occasionally use it as a bathroom," so as not to remind her of those times when, settling in for the evening, she starts laughing so uncontrollably while watching random Facebook videos on her phone that she pees right through to the mattress.

3. If she's really interested in living in less than 300 square feet with all the creature comforts (and here I am not referring to our cats), we can do so without the hassle of planning, permits, and construction. It's called an "RV." My brother-in-law has one so luxurious that it came with a butler.

Why hasn't someone developed a series about long-time married couples living in reasonably-sized housing and yet everything belonging to the husband is shoved to the back of the closet / refrigerator / bottom shelf? They could call it *I Live Here Too, You Know*. I'd watch that show. As long as a certain somebody stretched out next to me on the bed promises not to laugh.

I'm Not Your Stepping Stone

The phone rang shortly after noon one day last week. The display indicated the call was from my beloved wife, Carol, no doubt stealing a few minutes from her lunch break to express her profound affection for me.

"Hello, my dearest darling," I purred.

The voice on the other end of the line said, "I want you to check out this website that's all about things to do with rhubarb, watch an instructional video, make a list of the required materials, and pick them up this afternoon so I can get started on making some concrete stepping stones for the garden as soon as I get home from work."

After a brief pause, I replied, "Who *is* this?"

One of Carol's patients had brought her several big rhubarb plants. Her patient told her that, in addition to using the stalks for strawberry-rhubarb pie, the leaves -- which are "yuge" -- could be used to make a decorative impression in concrete. Carol, being a very crafty person (meaning, in this context, "arts and crafts"), was immediately intrigued and, as is her nature, wanted to get started on the project without delay.

I said sure, right after I finished what I was doing (which was dozing while watching *SportsCenter*, but I may have told her I was folding the laundry) I'd watch the video, compile the list, and -- if I *had* to -- spend a few hours wandering through the aisles of the hardware store. At this stage of my life, a trip to the hardware store brings almost as much titillation as a bachelor party's visit to a strip club.

I Googled the website, quickly viewed the video, assembled the list, and hit the road. The top priority, as you might imagine, was to purchase a bag of concrete. My only prior experience with this material was from slipping on it while running around our community pool as a kid. Little did I know that there are, like, EIGHT different kinds of concrete. I stood in front of the selections and tried to stream the video again on my phone to see if I could pinpoint which variety was used for this project, but inside the cavernous store I had no bars (unlike inside the cavernous strip club, which had three bars downstairs and two more in the VIP lounge), so I selected a package that looked vaguely familiar from my original viewing. I awkwardly muscled an 80-pound bag of concrete mix into my shopping cart. Shrugging off hernia symptoms, I then deadlifted a 50-pound bag of sand from the shelf. I think they call that move a "deadlift" because the effort nearly killed me.

After checkout, I managed to heave the load into the back of my car, launching a cloud of concrete and sand grit that covered every square inch of the upholstery. I lowered the windows and opened the sunroof, hoping to blow all the granules out on the drive home. The moment I merged onto the highway it started to rain, so I quickly closed up everything before the moisture had a chance to mingle with the concrete and form a rigid carapace around the seating in my Subaru.

It was clear again by the time Carol came home from work, and she was anxious to get underway. I wrestled the monstrous bags out of the car and into the wheelbarrow, stoically shedding only a few silent tears from the effort, and delivered everything to where she planned to tackle the creation of the decorative pieces. "OK -- I'm going to ~~take a nap~~ cut the grass," I announced. "Wait," she said. "Aren't you going to spread out the sand for me?" I wrangled the bulky bag of sand out of the wheelbarrow, sliced it open, and dumped it on top of her work table. "There you go. Have fun!" I headed toward the ~~soft and inviting living room couch~~ tool shed to retrieve the mower, getting only two steps away before Carol called to me again -- "What about the concrete?" "What about it?" I replied. She pleaded, "Can't you mix it up for me?" I let out a deep sigh while thinking to myself, "When did this become a joint project?" (I may have actually mumbled those words *sotto voce*, but I don't think Carol heard me.)

Now, as I said before -- I had no experience working with concrete. My knowledge of how to prepare it was limited to that brief video. It <u>seemed</u> simple enough - stir together concrete and water, in measured amounts, in a deep bucket using a big stick until it reached the proper consistency. As the weighty bag kept slipping from my grip, I guesstimated the amount to pour into the mixing bucket. The good news -- aiming for 40 pounds, my bucket weighed in at 39.5. That was close enough for me; I added the recommended amount of water to the dry contents and commenced stirring. Too late, I realized I should have used the wheelbarrow or a shallow container to mix it. That would have saved me thirty minutes and injuries to both wrists. It also would have resulted in far fewer profanities uttered during the process.

Carol came over to examine the finished slurry -- "Is it supposed to have rocks in it? The stuff in the video looked smooth, like cake batter." "Look," I steamed, "I bought the kind that looks like the bag in the video. I had no idea how many different kinds of concrete there are, or what their specific uses might be. If you want some other kind of concrete, then get in the car with me RIGHT NOW and we'll head back to the hardware store and you can pick out what you want." "No, I'll try it with what we've got here and if it doesn't work, then we'll try again another day."

I fervently hoped not to spend another minute, much less another day, on this project, but I nodded my assent. Dying for a towel to mop my sweaty brow and a cold ~~beer~~ drink of water, I headed toward the house. "Where are you going now? Aren't you going to make the stones with me?"

I'll cut to the end result: to our delight, the stones turned out just fine, whether or not we used the right kind of concrete or are still on speaking terms. The patterns are lovely and distinct; the contrast between the delicate imprint from the leaves and the solid mass of the concrete will make a striking addition to our garden.

I also learned a better way to deal with Carol's request for assistance with her next craft project: there's no harm in letting her call go to voicemail, giving me time to come up with a concrete reason why I can't participate.

Coil and Water

I am sitting at the table on our back deck, gazing at the lake and my surroundings on an absolutely glorious day. The sky is blue with billowy clouds. The water is undulating gently, stirred only by a slight breeze and the occasional surfacing of bass, trout, and pickerel.

We have a tall post in the yard, from which we hang an assortment of feeders in order to attract a variety of birds. Just this morning, while contentedly sipping my coffee, I've seen orioles, sparrows, blue jays, woodpeckers, goldfinches, nuthatches and, of course, chickadees.

Hey, what's that zig-zagging across the surface of the lake? Whoa, it's a snake! I can't really make out its size or what kind of snake it is.

Now there are swallows sailing around, snatching insects from the air with amazing speed and precision. One of them is diving toward the water -- uh oh, look out for that snake!

Hmm... now I don't see the swimming reptile. I wonder if it's decided to slither amongst the rocks stacked along the shoreline.

There goes an eagle soaring past, headed toward the island in the middle of the lake. I never fail to be amazed when I see an eagle; they're just so JESUS CHRIST! The snake is now in the yard...

"Calm down," I tell myself. There are no poisonous snakes found in the state of Maine, I have been assured. Of course, just because a snake isn't poisonous -- does that mean it won't bite you? Or do non-venomous snakes also have fangs? Wouldn't it still hurt like a son of a bitch if a regular snake bit you?

OK... I don't see the snake anymore; it must've gone back into the water. I can hear the distinctive cry of an osprey; let me step down from the deck and see if I can spot him overhead. Maybe he's returning to his nest in the woods, next to FUCKING HELL! THE GODDAM SNAKE IS RIGHT IN FRONT OF MY FEET!! I ALMOST STEPPED ON HIM!!!

Back on the deck, there is a hummingbird buzzing around the hanging flower pots, darting from one bright nectar-laden bloom to the next. I hope I don't scare it away since I'm now crouched atop the table, coffee spreading from the mug I knocked over when I jumped up. How can anyone be so sure there are *no* poisonous snakes in Maine? What if someone had a rattlesnake as a pet and it got loose and bred in the wild? I recall that rhyme I learned in Cub Scouts: "Red to black, venom lack / Red to yellow, kill a fellow." What am I supposed to do -- wait until this motherfucking snake bites me in the leg, and then, before he slithers away, snap a picture of him with my phone to show the EMTs so they know which kind of anti-venom to administer once they find me collapsed in the driveway with my airway swelling shut?

Look out, gentle mourning dove! There's a murderous snake hiding in the grass; don't come down to the ground to nibble on any of the seed that's spilled out of the feeders or else he'll dart up and crush your cute little head in the vise-like grip of his deadly jaws. Then he'll swallow you whole, I just know it.

I wish I had my long-handled metal rake handy, or a machete. Or maybe the chainsaw. I must remember to bring some yard tools along for protection the next time I go outside. If I ever go outside again.

I want to dash back into the house but am afraid to come down from the table, because what if the snake is lurking underneath? I think I can leap inside directly from my perch through the open door... oh, SHIT! The sliding screen is blocking my way. Ah, what the hell -- I can always replace it. Here I go...

Christ almighty... that screen is much tougher to barrel through than I thought it would be. Instead of giving way, it rebounds me ass over teakettle and now I'm flat on my back on the deck. I may also have a concussion. Let me lay here for a moment and try to clear my head. I don't think I'm bleeding anywhere, but boy does my OH DEAR GOD THERE'S THE SNAKE COILED UNDER THE TABLE RIGHT NEXT TO MY FACE!!!

Alright... now I'm back inside, with the deck door closed and locked behind me. As soon as I calm down a bit and change my underwear, I'll call to have a new patio screen installed. And then put the house on the market. This place is for the birds.

Clouds, island, lake and feeder post, as seen from the deck.
Snake lurking just out of frame, most likely.

Closing

If you've gotten this far, I commend you. In all honesty, I kind of skipped around after the first few pages – so my thanks to you for your perseverance.

You may have gleaned from these scribblings that we live on a lake in Maine. Although not life-long Mainers, we've quickly adopted the native lifestyle and are very thankful for our current waterfront location. Like a majority of Mainers – we respect the environment, we are rugged individualists, and we can't wait for Paul LePage's second term as Governor to come to an end.

John Donne famously wrote, "No man is an island." In the initial draft of that poem, his first line read, "No man is a septic tank" – but he kept at it and eventually came up with the catchier analogy. As I'm imagining Donne did, some of the posts in this book have been slightly revised from their initial versions. I'd venture to say they're improved from the originals, but that's for the reader to judge. In any event, I'm all donne with them now.

My thanks to the family members, friends, acquaintances and circumstances that inspired these musings.

And my greatest thanks go to my dear wife, Carol – my muse, my companion, my inspiration, occasionally a thorn in my side, but then again I'm no bargain either. She makes life worth living, especially when she bakes something delicious. Or on one of those rare occasions when, instead of rolling her eyes, she actually laughs at something I say.

Thank you for your interest in my second book. I'm already thinking about the third one, for which I envision the title as either *This One Is Funny -- I Swear*, or maybe *Amuse-bouche League*. Consider yourself warned.

\- Winthrop, Maine / July 2017

Discussion Points

1. The author makes frequent use of the word "flummox." Why is that? Do you think he knows what it means?

2. Presuming there is some truth at the heart of most of the entries in this book, why does the character of the author's wife ("Carol") put up with him? What benefits does she derive from dealing with his self-centered, petulant personality?

3. In "Sinking Relation-ship," the author describes himself as having "...thinning gray hair, wrinkles, sagging muscles and a paunch." Do you think he has completely let himself go by this point? Also, should there be a comma between "sagging muscles" and "and a paunch."?

4. List at least three things that bug the shit out of the author.

5. In "Are There Nuclear Codes for Launching an F-Bomb," the author includes this expression in French: *une seule langue n'est jamais suffisante*. What does this translate to in English? Would you please email the author to let him know?

6. Are the multiple references to "toilet" throughout the book an indicator of the author's anal-retentive personality? Or does he just scribble down a lot of these posts while sitting on the can?

7. If you could meet the author in person, how much would you pay for the opportunity? Checks are accepted.